When a shadow falls upon the Soul

By Ralph K. Jenkins

www.lightspira.com

Published by LightSpira, Sweden
www.lightspira.com

ISBN 978-91-86613-03-7

First issue, 2011

Author: Ralph K. Jenkins
www.verusanimus.com

Cover design by:
Marie Örnesved, LightSpira

Graphics and book design by:
Recito Förlag / Förlagsservice.se

When a shadow falls upon the Soul

Table of content

Introduction

To understand the nature of all energy forms is a major undertaking for anyone to study. When an individual decides to raise their consciousness it is by no means an isolated event, you are not alone. The very fact that you are now reading this is an indication that you have already embark upon a major chapter in your life experience. Welcome to the school of self-exorcism. Do not let this word *"exorcism"* alarm you, the word simply means that you are exorcising your right to transform or remove any negative energy that's not in harmony with your soul vibration i.e. love, light and joy. It could be as simple as *"think positively about whatever may seem negative"* because positive thought carries a high vibration of light.

Energy is everywhere, which is representative of *"the spirit of life."* The forces of dark and light fill and consume everything in existence. If you look at the words exorcism, exorcising, exhuming and existence they all have a common phenomenon i.e. the ex. For example "ex" is written in the Bible in the form of exodus, which is old Latin, from the Greek *exodus*: *ex-*, out. Ex is also used to describe ex-amount of goods. Yes, exorcism is exorcising your Divine right to be rid of any negative force or forces that are influencing your life. It is simply a thought away; for example it takes no more energy to think positively than negatively.

Thought is one of the most powerful forms of energy in the universe. It's an electrical charge that transiently expresses the light energy of your mental thoughts. The human being is a being of consciousness, of which there are three main levels that influence our spiritual development. The three levels of consciousness that are continually seeking to enhance the Divine within you are:

- 3D (D represents dimensional) consciousness is pure logic, the logical thinker i.e. the box thinker, represents the physical form.

- 4D consciousness is higher mind, the intuitive self. That of Spirit in action.

- 5D consciousness represents the opening of Soul guidance and the integration of your three higher senses with 3D and 4D on a daily basis.

When consciousness-raising occurs in any individual a major energy shift is taking place. There comes an inner calling towards seeking the meaning of life through the qualities of truth, love, joy and peace. This is the Soul's calling to harmonise itself with Universal Laws. The eye is turned inward to explore the meaning of the inner-self i.e. the energies that support physical life, those of the Spirit and Soul. From my own experiences, to grow spiritually is the main reason why the Soul decides to return to Earth i.e. to raise consciousness. The human race is sleeping, it has not yet fully woken to the inner love, joy and peace that is latent within. Soul calling is to serve other from the heart, where the ego does not rule and fear cannot control the physical form. The energy of higher consciousness is supreme.

I invite you to join me on a spiritual inner journey, and to explore the endless possibilities that life brings. Learning how to manage and use your energies in positive ways is a key towards liberating yourself from fears. By listening to your core being you will intuit and follow your inner-compass towards your spiritual pathway in life. True service to others can only be accessed when all forms of darkness have been transformed by Divine Light. It is only then, in your awakened state, that the lower nature cannot interfere with your service to others. May this book be an inspiration and a guide that assists you on your inner journey.

Chapter 1

Life Itself

Light is life and consciousness its expression. The physical body is primarily a receptor of energy through which divine[1] consciousness can be energised. There are different levels of consciousness that actively motivate the physical body. For example, when logical consciousness is activated towards others through the spoken word, the words used will impact the psyche to produce a positive or negative response. The energy of the words may impact the mental body, which may activate a purely logical response. Or the words may activate a negative force held in the emotional body, such as anger, and the person will respond emotionally.

What is the meaning of life?

Life is a conscious effort to express the divine will (loving peace) that is within all human beings. Everything you see around you has been created by thought. When this law is understood, you gain greater responsibility for your thoughts. Everyone is connected to a matrix of energy that follows universal laws. The law of action and reaction is one example, i.e. what you give or send out comes back to you in one form or another. Energy is everywhere and thought is one of the most creative, as well as destructive, energy forms. How a thought is applied determines the experiences we have.

---

1 God consciousness, love and light.

For me, one of the most important questions is, *What is my soul's journey and how can I serve others?* Let us explore the meaning of life in relation to the soul, spirit and physical body through the physical dualities and higher consciousness rising[2] that all human beings experience in everyday living. Consciousness rising occurs when an individual seeks universal truth through spiritual values[3]. Whenever universal values are established in an individual's consciousness that individual gains insight into the limits that logical perception imposes through the physical laws of time, distance and matter.

These are indeed deep times, where the blending of universal consciousness[4] is having a profound effect upon all levels of human thought. Consciousness is thought; thought is consciousness. Thought is a charged energy, a spark, a beam of light. It is an energy that must go somewhere, but where? Thoughts are as transient as universal consciousness. Telepathy is the means by which one person can read another's thoughts. This creative force has manifested our local universe and the galaxy in which the earth-world is held. The human form is born from light. First there was light, and then came the soul, followed by the lesser ethereal vibration of the spirit, to the dense energy of the physical body.[5] Light is the creative force of life. It is held within every being's heart and mind and is present regardless of how that person

2 A rising from third dimensional consciousness or 3D (logic or box thinking) into fourth and fifth dimensional thought (4D and 5D) i.e. an intuitive, non-judgmental, loving view of life.

3 Spiritual values are principles that support and expand life experiences - truth, love, joy and peace.

4 Universal consciousness is the source of truth, love, peace and joy, which represents the divine, the creator or God.

5 These are the three main bodies of energy that hold, activate and integrate the physical experiences we all have through the eight senses - five physical and three non-physical.

may be judged[6] to be. One of the universal laws states that everyone is equal; you are a mirror for me as I am for you. There is no right or wrong; there is only truth.

Universal consciousness is guiding the human race to expand all levels of communication. Managing and transforming lower consciousness, and developing your feelings and intuition to a level where inner struggle becomes inner peace are examples of consciousness rising. The human race has been accustomed to the concepts of darkness and evil, love and light, since the creation of Adam and Eve. Indeed, duality is to be found throughout all cultures and civilisations. The world of duality we live in allows us to understand the differences between good and bad, right and wrong. You would not be able to tell the difference between trust and jealousy if you had not experienced each of them and learned how to act in accordance to your truth. The experience jealousy provides will take you towards understanding the true nature of jealousy, which will eventually take you towards experiencing the opposite - self love.

The human race has been passing through duality for millennia. This "old consciousness" gave structure and meaning to life by clearly demonstrating opposites. Out of duality rose choice, which then led to judgement. These two concepts (choice and judgement) are largely responsible for much of the darkness that humanity is experiencing in the present day. Choice and judgement have fulfilled their meaning. Higher consciousness[7] is now opening the door of the logical mind to help us to understand how the concepts of goodness and evil come directly from the choices or judgements made about a

---

6 Judgment is not a universal law; it is a logical concept that the ego creates to justify itself.

7 Higher consciousness vibrates on the fourth dimension (4D+). Logic is third dimension (3D).

particular person or event, which can also expand into group ideology. The logical way of viewing the world is to see it as being black or white, right or wrong, and this thought pattern predominantly controls our choices. The core values of this pattern create the world we live in today.

Humans continue to kill each other in the name of judgement[8] and choice; it is no longer serving the greater good! In this context there is great importance in recognising the illusions that have been created and used through the development of fear. This fear[9] (other than basic survival fear) has deeply influenced and conditioned the consciousness of human beings for many millennia, and the fear that I refer to here is deeply embedded in our conditioning of *what to fear*, which has a strong link to the emotions and logical mind. Logical judgement is out of balance and is becoming increasingly destructive because of self-created fear. The logical mind has become too mental in its orientation. The ego and the darkness it holds have used fear as one of its main tools in order to take control of people's lives. Ego and fear continue to block your light and your truth by controlling your feelings[10]. This works if you are not being fully present and trusting.

Many masters of light have been trying to guide the consciousness of humanity towards greater awareness of how negative forces continue to manipulate the lower

8 Judgment is created by choice. Whenever you choose you have to compare one thing with another, which at the beginning gave humans the comparison of what was right or wrong and we acted accordingly. Judgment is not a universal law; it is a logical concept that the ego creates to justify itself.

9 There are two forms of fear, the basic survival fear that instinctively protects the physical body from harm, and the fear that the ego has created to protect its own interests.

10 Feelings are transformed emotions. Feelings emanate from the heart - emotions from the solar plexus.

mind and feelings. More people are now waking up to higher consciousness orientation. The Light Brotherhood has been guiding to provide opportunities for you to step into the unknown by learning to be present. In this manner, the awareness of spirituality is being activated through inner-spiritual will[11] (soul calling).

To study spiritual concepts, such as self-discipline, mindfulness and meditation is positive. Self-educating through books and esoteric workshops is another means of developing your spirituality. However the only true teacher is experience. If, for whatever reason, you fear experience then there is a control issue within you that needs to be transformed. This book will help guide you towards understanding what some of those issues are, what illusions of fear create and what evil is.

A large amount of knowledge and wisdom can be accessed from the seemingly endless books regarding this subject. Many esoteric teachings you may find are timeless, as truth is timeless. Universal laws resonate through the consciousness of light. *The human race is of the light. Each human being carries the seed of light from the creator. The Tree of Life symbolises this.*

Within all hearts is knowledge of what truth, peace, love and light are, because all human beings are of the light. You also intuitively know what is not of the light. There is the duality of evil and the goodness that runs deep in the human psyche. "The Dark and Light Brotherhood" is another term that describes beings of energy that are in a constant state of transformation. Although I refer to darkness as "evil", not all darkness contains evil. You

---

11 There are two forms of will. The first is the physical will that is motivated by logic i.e. not to fail or be seen to fail. The second will is the spiritual will that is being directed by its master the soul. The former takes energy from the physical body; the latter gives it energy.

can have a completely dark room that is void of any evil vibration. Many things can be hidden in darkness, but darkness is not actually void of light. There are differing bands of energy at work, as the word "brotherhood" may suggest, for light or dark, good or bad.

From where have these opposing forces appeared, and how or by who were they created? Why was the consciousness of human beings programmed to evolve through the concepts of logic and choice? Some argue that evil came from original sin and that goodness is our guiding light. But what do original sin and goodness actually mean?

Our local universe[12] is of vital importance for all human evolution. This universe is a portal to a far greater expansion of consciousness, that of the creator – God. The earth is held within a galaxy within a universe, a body within a body of energy. This, our local universe, is one of many universes that make up a greater body of consciousness. It is connected to twelve other universes or bodies of energy, making those thirteen universes a complete body of energy, which demonstrate the vastness of the creator's consciousness. On an energy level (metaphysical) the human body is literally a universe within a universe, a fact that most scientists find difficult to comprehend. This statement is both mind stopping and explosive at the same time because it goes against all sciences that are based on logic! The expansion of consciousness on any level requires a higher vibration of light to enter the conscious[13] field of an individual. The level of vibration

---

12 There are thirteen universes in all that make up the united body of universal consciousness. The earth resides within the third universe, the emotional aspect of the universal body.

13 There are nine levels of consciousness. The base consciousness emanates from the third-dimensional light frequency (3D), which holds the logical concepts of life.

of consciousness determines the density of its energy. If, for example, a person is very logical, then that person will be more fixed to earth laws (time, distance, matter and past, present and future) through the consciousness that is activated. However, if that individual's consciousness is more present in higher-consciousness orientation, then the consciousness used is that of trust and intuition. The first consciousness (logic, the left hemisphere of the brain) holds much fear; the second (intuition, the right hemisphere of the brain) holds the vibration of faith. From this simple explanation you may begin to grasp the gravity of universal laws.

Universal Laws creating Life

The human form is built upon the stardust of the universe. This is a summary of how Universal Laws create life on Earth to help raise the consciousness of mankind.

Universal flow of life: is the creative force of Light that gives access to seven levels of consciousness, three higher senses of Clairaudience, Clairvoyance, Clairsentience and the five physical senses.

The Human form in its Creation:

Light: Universal force of consciousness, wisdom, truth and love.

Soul: expression of the Universal force, the Divine.

Spirit: – server of the Soul, motivates the physical body.

Aura: subatomic energy force, Soul awareness, the higher personality, cosmic polarity.

Colour: light frequencies of Universal wisdom found within the Aura and chakras.

Etheric body: electromagnetic field of energy, an exact copy of the dense physical body. Is directly linked to the central nervous system.

Chakras: the receivers of colour codes that help to transform negative aspects of the physical body and mind.

Central nervous system: giving the life-force to the three aspects of the physical form.

Glands: receivers of information from the chakras, secretion of hormones.

Organs: the carrier of the information from the glands. The giver of life to the physical body.

Blood: the receiver of chemical information from the glands.

Physical body: the Temple of the Soul, Heaven and Earth, male and female, five physical and three higher senses, logic and intuition.

The following **Five Kingdoms** are each providing a foundation that enhances life on Earth:

Angel realm

Human Kingdom

Animal Kingdom

Plant Kingdom

Mineral Kingdom

In today's global consciousness there are an increasing number of people seeking to cross the bridge from 3D into 4D consciousness. In doing so they are, often unknowingly, establishing the higher consciousness vibration that will help them to transform their lower personality[14]. Crossing that bridge could involve acts as simple as deciding to meditate or start a discipline such as yoga or tai-chi. Consciousness is light, and when you actively work with these disciplines you automatically draw more light into your consciousness and cellular memory. Light has a positive effect on all areas of your psyche, particularly in the three glands that reside in the brain - the pineal, pituitary and carotid glands. Esoterically, these are seats of higher consciousness. Through the correct activation of the three major glands (for example by guided visualisation) your three higher senses (clairvoyance, clairaudience and clairsentience) will begin to establish themselves in your life by opening and developing the third eye and throat centres or chakras.

The psyche[15] of any individual is held together by universal forces that create the crystallised physical form. These rays of energy descend in a series of steps to embody the soul, spirit and the physical self into a temple of light, which are described on the pages that follow.

God consciousness: light.

Soul: the embodiment of light.

Spirit: the will of the soul.

The aura: a sub-atomic energy field that surrounds the entire physical body, the distance of which from the

---

14 The vibrations of the lower personality (ego) can hold the energies of fear, judgement and jealousy and tries to control it environment. The higher personality is the soul quality, which is the consciousness not influenced by the vibrations of the lower personality such as fear, judgment, jealousy or control.

15 The psyche refers to all energies that hold the physical form together, such as the aura, three higher senses and the five physical senses. When the psyche is fully functional, all eight senses are active. Intuition is one of the easiest energies to accept or recognise which is connected to the psyche.

physical body is determined by the light consciousness of the individual. It corresponds to the soul's impulses.

The etheric body: the blueprint of the dense physical body. The clairvoyant sees it as a light electromagnetic energy field that surrounds the entire physical form. It stands approximately seven to twenty-one centimetres away from the physical form. This energy field corresponds to the spirit that regulates the life force through the central nervous system, which is often referred to as chi or prana. The vitality of the etheric body is therefore of key importance for the well-being of the central nervous system. Within its field it can hold memories of past experiences and, at times, karmic injury. It is an important field to study when diagnosing illness, as it can be seen by the spiritual healer as a dark or grey area and it can help the healer to detect from where in the physical body the disease may originate. The etheric body may also hold karmic injuries that are felt as pain the physical body and the causes of which are undetectable by standard physiological means. Neither of these forms of injury (that often hold an element of physical pain) can be treated by medicine, as they are not physical in their nature. However spiritual healing has the means to heal such injuries. This is accomplished by transforming their vibration through the method of magnetic healing – the laying on of hands with the insight of higher senses.

The chakras: there are seven main chakras held within the physical body. These energy centres or seats of consciousness are individually fixed in certain positions - six of them run down the spinal column and the seventh resides just above the crown of the head. There is a lateral etheric web of energy that keeps each chakra in its exact position within the physical body. This web of energy also helps to prevent any leakage of energy from one centre to another, which can occur due to a shock or strong trauma. Starting from the top (number seven) the seven chakras are known as:

7: *The crown chakra:* located at the top of the head and representative of the higher consciousness, soul connection. This area holds the vibrations of all channels.

6: *The third eye* found in the centre of the forehead, resting between both physical eyes. I refer to it as "the window to the universe". It is the all-seeing eye and is responsible for clairvoyance.

5: *The throat centre:* found in the middle-lower neck. This centre relates to our abilities to speak and hear. It is responsible for our clairaudient faculty and the use of the sacred word.

4: *The heart chakra:* found within the heart region of the spine. This centre represents our love and compassionate aspects.

3: *The emotional body:* this centre is found about five centimetres below the belly button. It is a very strong and active centre in most people. It feels every vibration within its environment and responds accordingly and is responsible for our emotional state.

2: *The sacral chakra:* this centre is found seven centimetres above the pubic bone. It is responsible for reproduction and how we identify with our sexuality, as well as the male and female aspects of our psyche.

1: *The root chakra:* this centre acts as a foundation stone upon which a person can build their life principles. When generally closed it keeps the psyche in the 3D. When awakened it becomes like a mirror that reflects the light from the crown chakra back up through the chakra channels, in an effort to clear all that hinders spiritual progress. It is the negative polarity, whilst the crown chakra is the positive aspect. It is important to help ground the psyche as 4D consciousness-awakening occurs through the physical temple. It holds the basic life principle.

Each chakra can be seen as a disk of energy that has a hole in the middle – you could imagine it as a CD. When the chakras are being awakened, the higher consciousness (light) will pass down through each chakra to reach the bottom or root chakra from where it will rise in an effort to awaken and stimulate each chakra's consciousness. It effectively seeks to remove and transform any vibration that is not in harmony with that of the soul. This helps to unite the force of all seven chakras. The higher force - light, is known as the *fire of kundalini*, of which there are three fires.[16] As the energy of kundalini passes through each chakra, it carries codes of colour consciousness that will strike the bottom root chakra in order to make it rise again. As the energies rise, they will draw anything that is impure through with them (such as negative thoughts and feelings). This is in an effort to transform the impurity, which at times can be seen by the healer. For example, you may be holding on to another person's feelings which may be interfering with your own. Those negative feelings can then be transformed into light consciousness by the healer or the self. Such an impurity could be a thought of anger, jealousy or a judgement of another person. The vibration of such consciousness is in some way connected to the original evil that may have a strong link to your emotional body as the receiver or sender.

Each chakra is a metaphysical energy that is fundamentally and responsibly connected to a specific gland.

---

16 Fire of friction, physical. Fire of electric spirit and etheric body and atomic fire, soul and cosmos.

Through (positive or negative) stimulation of the gland, it is then able to direct the cocktail of hormones throughout the physical body. All energy forms come from somewhere in order to give life. An example of this, on a metaphysical level, is how the heart chakra stimulates a positive or negative energy into the thymus gland, or how the throat chakra resonates with the thyroid gland to produce good health or otherwise. These two examples have a definite effect on physical well-being through direct consciousness orientation. This is an example of how bridges are built between esoteric and physical sciences to create deeper understanding through holistic methods of treatment, where the relevance of the spirit and soul are added to any form of analysis.

As light enters the metaphysical bodies of the aura it lowers its vibration to a sub-atomic level, which makes it possible for the lower vibration of light - colour - to be present. From there, the life force is able to enter the etheric body, which then drops its vibration to an electromagnetic field, which can have a positive effect upon the central nervous system. The various irrational codes of colour are then able to pass up and down the entire chakra system; these colour-coded energies have a definite effect upon the physical apparatus. Through their vibration they touch all aspects of physiological makeup, right down to the cells and micro-organisms. Chemical codes are created and produced by the direct influences that the chakras have over the glands, thus affecting our body chemistry. All of this occurs due to consciousness awareness.

It then stands that the entire physical form and its psyche is polarised through the root and crown chakras. This greatly aids the flow of electromagnetic energy therein, as in the etheric colours that have an effect upon the chakras and glands. When the light force of the kundalini strikes the root chakra, it is mirrored back up through the entire chakra system and out through the crown chakra. This is what the flow of kundalini rising represents. It provides an opportunity for the transformation of negative energies to occur. The chakras are purely receivers, holders and transmitters of energy, as is the etheric body.

The glands: there are seven main glands that are directly connected to the seven main chakras. They are as follows:

Pineal: to the crown chakra.

Pituitary: to the third eye and carotid gland.

Thyroid: to the throat centre.

Thymus: to the heart chakra.

Pancreas: to the solar plexus.

Gonads: to the sacral centre.

Adrenal: to the base chakra.

Esoterically speaking, each chakra and gland is directly responsible for the chemical information that flows into the bloodstream. Negative thinking can have a strong effect upon the stimulation and stability of each gland. Another example is that when the thyroid gland is not functioning properly, the flow of thyroxin is affected. This can create a variety of problems throughout the physical body, such as sleeplessness, anxieties and various states of doubt and confusion. Medical interventionists may prescribe doses of thyroxin in an effort to counteract or replace the natural ability to produce thyroxin. This merely deals with the symptoms and not the cause of the imbalance! An in-depth examination of the individual may reveal certain characteristic traits relating to this particular type of imbalance and a possible cure. It may be that the individual is confused about life in general, resulting in their being unable to maintain a positive outlook and they are therefore less likely to make positive decisions. They may also lack the motivation to take charge of their affairs, relying upon others instead. They tend to look outward for answers instead of going inwardly. The throat chakra symbolically indicates that they may lack the power to express themselves, other than through anger. These are symptoms that are related to thyroid imbalances.

The human being is a creation of consciousness, and every human being can change their life patterns by activating right thinking. Each gland in the physical body is connected to a specific chakra, which is connected to the source, that of light.

The light I refer to here is not of the same magnitude to that of physical light, or sunlight. It is of a far greater magnitude which is why it is undetectable by physical means – it is the unseen light. The light of higher consciousness goes far beyond physical boundaries because it emanates from the fourth dimension upwards.

The organs: each organ is connected in one way or another to a specific gland, as are the glands to a chakra. For example, the adrenal gland is connected to the kidneys and the kidney is ruled by the solar plexus chakra. If you study human anatomy in relation to each chakra, you will find its relationship to a particular organ. The organs are like the machines of a factory, which require a certain amount of maintenance. Each organ has its own particular vibration (this is witnessed with organ transplants, where an organ will be rejected by the body of the person receiving it due to it having a different vibration to the original organ and body it now finds itself in). The organs help to push, move, clear and remove impurities from the physical body. The heart helps to pump the blood along our arteries and veins. Certain organs work to clean the blood whilst others digest food intake through a mixture of acids and node[17] activity to help balance and extract what is required by the physical body. It is a beautiful and efficient creation.

The largest area of organs that is covered by a single chakra is the solar plexus. This centre rules the whole abdominal area. There is a commonly used phrase, "You are what you eat." This statement is misleading. I prefer to say, "You are what you feel or think you are." You could eat the purest food, but if your mental or emotional state is not in harmony, that food will not be digested properly. Many people miss this important point. Mental and emotional stability is crucial for well-being and I believe this is very clearly shown by the increasing numbers of those who contract bowel cancer and allergies.

Stress is another major contributory factor to cancer. This is because the solar plexus is the most highly sensitive area in present-day consciousness – the two are linked. The solar plexus is a body of energy that is often referred to as the emotional self. This energy field feels every vibration and reacts to it accordingly. If a person's life principles are emotionally-based, then he or she is more likely to develop an illness through the stress factor related to that area. Diabetes is an example that is possibly related to bitterness in life that has not been resolved and healed from within the individual. Again we come back to the all important point of finding the cause.

Treating the symptoms merely serves to delay the change required. Taking away the organ changes nothing; what

---

17 Part of the lymphatic system.

is important is to find out why the organ has reached the stage of needing invasive surgery. Can the organ be healed or treated before such a drastic step is required? In my opinion, removal of an organ is opposite to healing. It is similar to changing the food to suit the allergy. The basic issues must be addressed in order for conscious physical change to occur. For example, you might ask yourself the question, "Why do all organ implants require medication to prevent rejection of the implanted organ?" For me the reason is clear. The psyche of the organ receiver knows that an alien organ has arrived, and all body energies (such as cells) try to reject it because it has an alien vibration. To a great degree medicine has overcome such difficulties on the physical level through drug intervention and prevention, but what about the psyche? Prevention is possible in all of these areas of disease, but this requires greater knowledge and understanding of the metaphysical realities as I, and an ever increasing number of others, see them demonstrating.

The blood: is, as we know, the carrier of life and nourishes the physical body. Oxygen, saline, haemoglobin, plasma and a concoction of hormones are relayed around the entire body via the bloodstream, and this supports life as we know it to be.

The flow of blood is dependent upon two principles; the first being the electromagnetic field of the etheric body, and the second the heart itself. Here lies another duality in our life system. The heart requires electrical stimulation in order for it to pump blood through the arteries and veins. That stimulation comes from what I term the "universal heartbeat." The universal heartbeat is felt by sensitive people in their psyche as waves of energy. These waves of energy fall upon our shores to resonate with the etheric body which passes its force onto and through the central nervous system. This is the electrical impulse that all humans feel. It creates the flow of the heart beat and the heart holds the strongest electrical impulse within the physical body.

The physical body has two important secondary pumps which help the blood to circulate. The first being etheric sleeves which are around all veins and arteries (it is said that the physical form holds some 80,000 kilometres of veins). The etheric sleeve helps to pump the blood around the physical body by holding a positive charge of energy, whilst the blood holds a negative charge. These forces act like the two poles of a magnet. If you try to push the same poles together, great resistance occurs. However, when opposite ends connect the positive charge of the etheric energy helps to push the negative energy of the blood along.

The third pump is our feet. When we walk or run the impact of the feet on the ground acts like a pump, aiding blood circulation. This is why walking, jogging and running are deemed to be so good for general health and blood circulation.

The bones: these form the skeletal structure which helps to give the individual appearance of the physical form. In any given lifetime the physical body is seeking perfection through our interaction with it, which is partly why we choose our parents for their DNA and body type. Our bones are in a constant state of renewal and transformation; they evolve and hold information regarding our health and wellbeing.

The cells: science states that the physical body is made up of some seventy trillion cells. Each cell is a nucleus of energy which communicates with other cells within their environment and the physical body as a whole. The way we think and feel has a definite impact upon every cell in our body. For example if you think negatively, your consciousness touches every cell with a negative vibration. The opposite is also true, which is why the positive thinker generally feels uplifted. This is because more light enters its domain through the consciousness. The greater the light a person attracts (through positive thought), the stronger the life force; the stronger the life force the greater the power to manifest egoless wishes, dreams and visions.

Esoterically speaking there is something that is recognised as *cellular memory,* where each cell has an ability to hold memory. An example is when a person has a major organ transplant such as the heart or kidney. The person receiving the transplant will actually take on board the other person's personality (their vibration). It could be soon after the implant that their preference of diet may take on another meaning for them, such as a desire for meat which was not present before. Their personality may also change, such as becoming more angry or aggressive because the implant holds the memory of anger. The part of the anatomy where a person may be holding onto a negative memory or feeling, will in part, determine the effect it has. If you were brought up to be pessimistic and fearful, a lot of emotional force can be stored. This can be quite a strong energy to transform. Here again, positive or negative attitudes to life can play a major role in health. I believe, from experience of following my own spiritual practice and development, that it is important to clear and transform any negative cellular memories you may have. It is also true to say that those feelings are often not yours; someone may have given them to you in the form of thoughts which must be cleared in order to find your own true vibration.

The skin: this is the largest organ of the physical body, and has three layers:

1: *The epidermis:* The outermost layer of the skin protects the body from the environment. Its thickness varies from .05 mm on the eyelids to 1.5 mm on the palms and soles of the feet. It is made up of five sub-layers that work together to continually rebuild the surface of the skin.

2: *The dermis:* This layer is located beneath the epidermis and is the thickest of the three layers of the skin (1.5 to 4 mm thick). It accounts for approximately ninety per cent of the thickness of the skin and its main function is to regulate temperature and to supply the epidermis with nutrients. Much of the body's water is stored within the dermis. This layer contains most of the skin's cells and structures, which include blood vessels, lymph vessels, hair follicles, glands, sebaceous glands, nerve endings, collagen and elastin.

3: *The subcutis:* this is the innermost layer of the skin. It consists of a network of fat and collagen cells. The subcutis is also known as the hypodermis, and functions as an insulator to help conserve body heat. It also acts as a shock absorber to protect the inner organs. It stores fat as an energy server, and the blood vessels, nerves, lymph vessels and hair follicles cross through this layer. Its thickness varies with each individual.

The skin has many vital functions, including to hold and protect what lies beneath it. It acts as a secondary lung; it absorbs what is in its environment. It is highly sensitive to touch. It is the chief organ that regulates the body temperature by sending messages through the central nervous system to either greatly limit or increase the blood flow to any given area in the body. It does this to maintain a core temperature. This is part of the survival infrastructure of the human being that has evolved over millions of years.

Skin is highly receptive to light; vitamin D is created in the body by exposing the skin to sunlight. Our skin is also extremely receptive to vibrations and forces which touch and affect our intuitive psyche. For example, you can use your hands to feel another person's vibration without physically touching them. This may be help you to understand whether they are in a positive or negative frame of mind and may tell you that the emotional body of an individual is in a state of stress or depressed.

A simple way of proving that you have a psychic touch is to get a friend or relation to stand in front of you with a distance of about two yards between you. Raise both hands up in front of you with your palms facing the other person. Close your eyes for a moment and take a few deep breaths to help centre yourself by letting go of any tension you may feel in the body. Focusing on your hands and the feelings around them, slowly move forwards to the other person and keep the levels of your hands at the same height. Try to feel or make contact with the electrical field – aura and etheric body - that surrounds you both. As you draw closer to the other person and their hands you may begin to feel warmer in your body and hands. When you are about two feet away from the other person's hands, stop. Then gradually push your hands forward towards the other person's hands. At this point try to feel if there is subtle resistance to your hands moving forward. Your hands may also feel much warmer at this point. This is due to the presence of the etheric body's electromagnetic field. As you push your hands closer, to about twelve or fifteen centimetres away, you may definitely feel electromagnetic energy - to the extent that you feel that you cannot move them forward. Your skin may feel electric and tingle slightly. This for me is a form of proof of the metaphysical force of the electric field we all have.

The skin is in a constant process of renewing its outer layer; the entire epidermis is changed approximately every twenty-seven days. It is the third most important protective field of energy, the first two being the aura and the etheric body. The skin is also the chief reflector of what is going on internally, due to its close connection to the central nervous system and the glands. *The condition of all forms of eczema is a good example of how the skin reflects back to say that something within is out of order, help!*

Eczema and allergies are on the increase, which I feel has a lot to do with the general disorder of the emotional body, central nervous system and glands, as well as what we take in via cosmetics, orally and atmospherically. All have a bearing upon the health of the skin.

The vital bodies of energy that support the physical body:

Below is a list of energy forms that hold and keep the physical body intact by uniting the life forces of spirit and soul. From an esoteric point of view it is the soul that keeps the physical body alive. The soul determines when it is to return to its original source[18] through physical death, which I see as rebirth. The soul's departure occurs in a variety of ways, which are related to a person's karma or life process and ongoing experiences. This is

---

18 Returning to your home place in this universe or another universe, which could be to another world in another galaxy.

in total contrast to the attitude of conventional medicine which puts so much emphasis on the preservation of the dense physical body at all costs. Classical science gives little or no recognition to the qualities of the spirit and soul. In my experience, this is clearly seen in the area of coma patients, where the soul's journey is not recognised as an integral part of the life and death process. We all play our part in revealing the truth of spiritual science and the universal laws in relation to life-giving forces. Let us rejoice by continuing to spread the word through our insights and experiences which go beyond the logical mindset. For this to come about, higher consciousness has to be activated in order to understand the esoteric sciences of spirit and soul. The list given below could help you to assess the various life forces through and is derived from my experiences and understanding of what creates the physical form.

The physical body is created and supported by the following:

1. The soul

2. The spirit – the server of the soul

3. Subtle bodies of mind (here I explain three levels of mind) and the emotions which are simply qualified as energy centres.

4. The vital body with its seven major centres (chakras).

5. The central nervous system; which has three divisions.
   - The life force
   - The quality of energy
   - The etheric body

6. The endocrine system (glands) in relation to the chakras. These are the controlling factors of health or ill-health of the physical form.

7. The vital organs.

8. The bloodstream.

9. The physical body, the temple of the above. The server of the spirit and soul.

If you listen and tune into the light of your soul, your spirit will guide you through the inner conflicts that logic, the ego and emotions create. The ego and emotions create conflicts by separating you from your truth, your source of love. Anger and negative thinking are such dark energies. What is outside of you is simply a reflector, a message that seeks to guide you towards your inner journey. And for that to be established, you cannot take anything personally. If you do then your ego is in control. Here lies another basic truth - what is hidden cannot be of the light. Evil uses darkness to create fear in order to elude. It keeps you from the light of truth. It continually seeks to delude reasoning by creating doubt in order to keep you in darkness. Fear is such an illusion. Corruption, fear and evil were created by a singular high being to control and manipulate those disciples that were held under that particular vibration. This occurred at the very early start of the second initiation i.e. the moving of energy (kundalini) upwards from the first chakra to the second. This negative vibration is known as "evil." The evil spread amongst many of the souls that were under the guidance of this particular master. Their souls became corrupted by the ego, and fear was created to block the heart of love. The ego-based lower personality was then created. The higher personality is soul-based, and of truth, light, peace and joy, which is still present in all beings, and is continually seeking ways in which to transform the darkness.

When the Masters of Light discovered the Master of Darkness, many souls were banished from this universe by the Godhead. These beings have no connection to their heart and its vibration, and are totally void of feeling. Over many centuries the corrupted beings manipulated the feelings of others for their own gain, and in this manner the original evil spread through the people. They took rather than gave. They chose to control rather than release. They wanted to take the very soul vibration of a light turning it into darkness. In this manner evil found ways in which to keep the global consciousness in the dark. Those that were banished by the Masters of Light I call the "greys". This is the basis of the "original evil." Greys do not reincarnate – they are unable to due to their expulsion from this universe. The only way they can return is by means of possession. At this juncture there are very few greys actually present on earth (I have known three personally); their power is diminishing and they are dying out.

Universal laws are timeless and exacting. After the banishing of the corrupt master, the laws of karma and choice were brought forth by the Godhead into the consciousness of all human beings. This was achieved in order to transform the original evil. But it must be said that universal laws work as equally for evil as they do for light, but with a fundamental difference. Evil uses fear to control and destroy, and the latter's (light) role is to release and create.

Chapter 2

The Law of Karma and Choice

The law of karma[19] was created along with choice (choice being a logical orientation) in order to transform the third dimensional consciousness of logic into higher mind principles. Original evil still persists and has a certain amount of control over the earth's population through 3D orientation. Within the orientation of lower mind, resides an energy form that is known as "ego". This energy form is derived from the consciousness of the original evil, and as such continually seeks to keep the individual away from their light, truth and love. The shadow of the ego's body achieves this through creating energy forms such as fear, deceit, lies, hatred, racism, murder and judgemental attitudes. Through the activation of the Law of Karma and choice, the reflections of both evil and good can be seen for what they truly are. Through working with karma you have the opportunity to transform any negative forces that you have built into your life cycles over the many lifetimes that you have lived on earth. The old consciousness of fear and control will no longer be able to prevent you and humanity from raising consciousness.

---

19 Karma is the law of repaying; the law of cause and effect through choices made. There is positive karma just as there is negative. It can be an act committed for either wanting, having or needing something. If, for example, you are strongly negative to someone, it stands that it will return to you in order to give you opportunity to change your behavior patterns. Likewise, you may be positive towards others and others will return your kindness.

The shadow world,[20] underworld[21] and dark brother-hood,[22] are words I use to describe negative forces. These are slowly being transformed by the development of a greater sense of integrity with pure intent in all that we may do. By following this path, humanity at large is freeing itself from the force of the original evil. When the individual steps into the light of higher consciousness (4D), faith[23] is born. Whenever an individual embarks upon the path of spiritual development, he or she will be the creator of good karma. Whenever consciousness is orientated towards thinking and living through higher mind principles with right intentions, love and light is present, and evil is not.

It is essential to understand for the great majority of people who are experiencing ill health, acute disease and death, their conditions are related to their karma. A particular incarnation is not an isolated event in the life of the soul, but it is nevertheless a part of the wholeness of a person's experience. The consequent sequences of experience that we have in any given lifetime are in-tended to lead towards greater awareness of the choices we make. These choices will eventually lead to decision making that will help direct us towards a clearer goal in life. Choice will lead to deciding; deciding is not based on viewing the world as black or white. When you make a decision you are not involved in the drama or seeing yourself as a victim, you are observing what is taking place from a neutral position – from across the river. From there you can decide what to do next without the interference of judgement or fear.

---

20 All that is hidden.

21 A realm where dark and evil beings coexist.

22 An established order of dark masters that continually seek to control others.

23 A knowing of what is true. A deep trust in the unknown, accepting what is to come without fear.

When you have recognised a clear intent, you may then be able to move forward by deciding to take positive steps in order to create good karma. By living a life through positive thinking, right intentions, integrity and living in truth, you will guide yourself to liberate the self from the ego's hold. Your spirit seeks full liberation of body and soul, each of which has deep karmic links with the intuitive aspect of each person.

Not every soul which has returned to the earth has been drawn here under the pull of karmic debt. There are many who are here with no karma to transform; they are here to serve on a deeper level.

The aims and goals that any new spiritual student faces are liberation and freedom from the lower mind. It is chiefly the three lower chakra centres (root, sacral and emotional) that control the physical life, which is where the ego and emotional self seek to influence and corrupt initial feelings. It must be stated that the logic (lower mind), ego (identity) and the emotional body (needs) are deeply influential in what you may choose to do in any given situation (if you are caught up in your emotions). The idea here is to move out of the realms of the purely selfish "I" into something which is much wider in its outlook, i.e. genuine concern for others. Here the power of the word "liberation" is more often spoken in the terms of "liberty". Liberty, in the minds of many, means freedom from the way humanity uses man-made laws to control and rule others. The old vibration of controlling others through the ego's choices and lower-mind orientation has reached a point of stagnation. Judgement is not truth, nor is it light: it is ego-based. Judgement is deeply connected to choice that serves its master, the ego. Choosing is connected to how you have come to view your outer world through your needs and desires.

Through choosing, you restrict your love, because you are making preferences between one and another (I prefer this, not that). Whenever you do this, you cannot love because acceptance is not present. Therefore liberty is also not present because your thoughts are conditioned. These very thoughts are connected to the original darkness.

It is clear to see how the lower nature (ego and emotion) can create a line of descent that often leads into negativity. Historically, this same lineage has led world leaders into many documented wars. The same lineage of thought is still present in today's consciousness and it continues to create and feed the ego's desire for attention through attack. The lower nature holds the egoism that humanity continues to struggle with. It is continually seeking to control and destroy the very world we live in, in order to maintain its identity. But humanity is beginning to wake up to the fact that individually we have a responsibility towards the whole world; truth must be expressed and acted upon. This can only be done by transforming the fears and control that the ego has over the psyche and by taking positive steps towards higher consciousness orientation. You do not have to create higher consciousness, you already have it. You have been asleep, but are now awakening!

Through choice, logical thought created the rules that have built the societies we live in today. However during this critical Aquarian period, humanity is seeking higher-mind principles. Integrity and intuition are words that are being used more frequently in business and corporate circles. The laws and rules of higher consciousness may seem difficult to understand from the logical perspective. This is because the ego has a strong hold over your inner feelings. For example, enacting a simple rule of accepting and respecting another person's point of view is one way of making real change happen! You can befriend another with such an attitude. Our differences are compatible, as long as they are not viewed as personal. Through developing inner acceptance, judgement is not attached, and then true value will be added to your decision making. The ego's wishes are to separate you from your love and light by saying to you that the other party will not succeed, that you must fear it - the unknown. The ego seeks to justify its identity to rule your life through fear of loss.

Acceptance leads to you being fully present, then compassion can enter your heart, and compassion leads to freedom of mind and emotions because acceptance follows the path of liberty. Liberty creates a free flow of energy where there is no resistance to life itself. Through acceptance you decide to live and experience life through higher-mind principles of right thinking. This is as it should be, provided that your wishes, choices, thoughts and desires are free from selfish thinking. Generally speaking, on a global consciousness level, higher-mind principles are not as yet being manifested by the majority. This is due to the way in which the world has been viewed through old theories and judgement and material needs that have been passed down from generation to generation. A distinct lack of understanding and insight into what evil is, and how it is created and maintained, stems from those who are in positions of power.

Fear is such a controlling factor and those in power often use it to control others. Fear blocks your spiritual development; it is a dark force. The old consciousness of choice allowed the thinker to see the world from the outside as being black or white. It is true that this gave direction and meaning to the choices made, but at what cost? In today's climate of rising global consciousness, those choices and judgements are the killing fields. They come in the guise of politics and religious idealism and there seems no end to the corruption that follow. Until higher-consciousness thought patterns take place, the lower consciousness will continue to dominate. Oneness[24] is your goal - not separation. Truth, acceptance, equality and compassion are the powers of true liberty. These are the opposite vibrations to that of the ego, which will tell you these are pain not joy!

If you go deeper into understanding the word liberation, you will begin to find your truth, which must come from within you. You hold the answers to liberate yourself from the ego and lower nature. It is not outside of you, which is why it is important to understand the meaning of not taking anything personally! Your sense of freedom will move you along certain predetermined lines (predetermined by the soul understanding), which lead you along a path of least resistance. Trust your inner feelings, because this will awaken your power to express your divinity. You are capable of individually and collectively expressing your divine self. The collective is group consciousness, as we often attract others into our fold through past karmic experiences. A society, region - or indeed a nation - can also harvest **good karma** by being present through divine awareness of worldly affairs. Everything is connected!

In the history of the last two thousand years there have been four great symbolic happenings that have aided the transformation of darkness and evil. This has come through the realisation and enactment of **liberalisation,** and not simply **liberty**. As history demonstrates, those who have the eyes to see, and the ears to hear, along with

---

24 A united body of thought, that of selflessness, joy, love and peace.

the mind to interpret, will have felt the effects of these great past moments. These great moments in history sought to transform (consciously or unconsciously) negative karma through their positive creative force, they are:

1: The life of Jesus Christ who taught us much about evil, eternity and karma.

2: The signing of the Magna Carta.

3: The abolition of slavery in general, which to a degree in today's societies has moved from shackles to materialistic slavery!

4: The liberation of humanity through the United Nations movement.

Those who are in a position to choose war over peace are or have been strongly connected to the original evil. Whenever a negative step is taken (war), it is a means of expressing and delivering the negative forces of evil, which can affect thousands, if not millions of people. Such a soul was that of Hitler, whose consciousness is still kept alive today because humanity has not yet learned to let go of those past experiences and feelings. Humanity recreates the karma of Hitler's consciousness by reliving it through holding annual memorial services. This helps to keep the dark psyche of those times trapped on the earth, from where the anger and hatred of what happened during those dark years is rekindled or brought out into the world consciousness again. Year after year this is done. This is an example of how the old way of thinking works - by holding onto the past it is trapped in its own time zone. Reality is that it cannot be changed or altered in any way.

Logic lives in the past as a means of identity and this only serves to keep the old consciousness alive. If you live much of your life in the past, then you cannot experience the magic of life in the present moment. If you are not present you will not experience life with joy and peace in mind and heart. Is humanity ever going to move on? It is not that we are not meant to remember, but there are also positive events or happenings in our lives.

The past cannot be changed or altered, but each individual is collectively responsible for what is created through thought. Thoughts enter the collective consciousness and manifest what you create and experience in your life! You are the creator of everything you have received in your life, because on some level you have asked for the experience.

The aspect of karma involves the three aspects of human evolution, which are:

1: The physical world.

2: The world of emotion and desire.

3: The mental plane.

What is really happening through the law of karma in relation to the life of the individual, of humanity and in the lives of nations? It is from here that a tremendous shift of consciousness is taking place (through spiritual involvement) to put right the effects of the *ancient original evil*. The law of karma is affecting everyone whether they are consciously or unconsciously aware of such a law. There is no separation between those who feel that they are on a spiritual journey and those who do not, because consciously all beings make up the collective consciousness of the world and the universe. The choices and decisions each individual makes activate the laws of cause and effect, action and reaction. These are natural laws that seek to release the power of the original evil by giving the experiences that individuals and groups

44

require to take them into the light. The reasoning of one's consciousness is a complex matter to understand due to the many connotations therein. But ultimately it is down to each person, the nation and the international world that has produced the effects under which humanity today experiences life. The human being is a conscious being of immense possibilities. Which consciousness you are now activating determines the experiences that you attract and how you view the world.

The law of karma has been treated with great scepticism in the Western world. But karma is a fact of life in other cultures, particularly in the Buddhist and Hindu traditions. However the concept is now gaining greater recognition as a truism that is gradually being considered more deeply in relation to all human affairs. For example if you steal something from another person, the Law of Karma states that something will be stolen from you, i.e. the mirror effect. Many may refer to it by another name, but in today's world karma is reaping what was sown some time ago. The human memory tends to be short and many do not recognise that what they receive is due to the Law of Karma.

Karma is the brother of truth – truth is the sister of life. Truth is pure in its essence and cannot be changed or altered in any form. Corruption is a dark energy that is often hidden in the form of a lie; both seem to be endemic in our cultures. Truth will eventually be recognised by all beings as a saviour of the self. A person's integrity is based on truth, which is used as a basis of life itself.

The earth, galaxies and universe resonate through the consciousness of God. Within its vibrations (light force) are held an unimaginable variety of codes that are enacted every second of every day to help raise the consciousness of humanity. To a great degree, many of these vibration forces formulate as crystallised forms, the physical body being the most obvious form of a crystal-lisation of light. Others can be seen as material things such as a car, house, cup, water or others that are present in the four lower kingdoms of mineral, plant, animal and human. All energy forms are serving humanity by providing the basics of life.

To a great degree, the consciousness of humanity func-tions through logic or third-dimensional thought and this corresponds to the laws of linear time, distance and matter. Every soul is a matrix of higher consciousness that is vibrating on the fourth and fifth dimensional consciousness. The developing individual human being at times receives an update of higher vibrations via their natural channel, which is connected to the universal consciousness. Sometimes an initiate can feel and hear the incoming code as a high-pitched tone in one ear. It is as if the hardware on your computer (mind) is being updated. This update is to keep your soul in line with the continuing expansion of universal consciousness. I refer to universal consciousness expansion as the "greater plan". This was evoked many millions of years ago by the creator God, who for me is the definitive provider of consciousness, "I am in all things whilst at the same time I am nothing!"

Many valuable experiences are created by those whose lives are based on 3D consciousness. If, for example, you choose what suits your ego best, you will also fill yourself with the needs and desires of your lower nature. Those choices may seem right – as the ego will tell you they are – but all choices are based on logical tempera-ments that can be, and often are, clouded by emotional responses to choices made. When the path is set by your choices and decisions, each determines how you may or may not follow your natural spiritual path. Remembering each thought you have has a definite effect upon the environment at large; we are all intricately connected to the oneness of all things i.e. consciousness. It is as if we are all being held within a ball of wire that caries our electrical impulses or neuron transmitter into terminals. These create the consciousness web of the earth.[25]

An individual being may spend a lifetime following a path and encountering many difficulties. These could be experienced as marital loss, divorce, job failure, financial difficulties or not having a holiday. Everything that appears in a person's life has in fact come to strengthen the soul's resolve and to follow the original experience-orientated path; some may call this karmic growth. Karma is enacted through 3D consciousness of choice, but is directed from the fourth plane of consciousness that gives substance to the choices you make. Choice vibrates with the five physical senses, logical mind and the emotional body. The choices we make have a definite effect upon the seven main chakras, but chiefly the three lower chakras are under the influences of the ego and the emotional vibrations therein. These forces can and do corrupt[26] the higher chakra centres, as well as consciousness itself (3D).

Ultimately, the human being is following a path of consciousness expansion by crossing the bridge from 3D into 4D consciousness. But there are few who are in harmony with their 5D consciousness. Whenever the spiritual path is opened by an individual, consciousness rising occurs in their life and they are on a path of no return. When

25 Every human being plays a part in raising global consciousness; everyone is a transmitter of light.

26 Negativity, such as judgment and darkness, is created.

47

acceptance is developed as a basic principle of spiritual truth in your life, then you become present and follow the path of least resistance.

Humanity as a whole has passed through the first two initiations. The first initiation was a rising of consciousness from pure survival instincts (root chakra) into beings of reproduction i.e. mating (second chakra), thus drawing more souls to earth. This helped to transform the second chakra or sacral centre. The human race now stands firmly in the emotional state of energy transformation, from 3D into the 4D. This basically means that the ego, fears and emotional discord are being transformed by being open to higher consciousness activity.

Chakras, of which there are seven, are metaphysical light energy centres of consciousness held within the physical organism. It stands that the polarity of the life force (an electrically charged light) runs from the crown of the head (crown chakra) through the spinal column (which is where the remaining five main chakras are to be found) down to the coccyx. The coccyx grounds the life force in the physical body.

Each chakra is deeply connected to the physical body that guides and directs the life force of chi. The root chakra centre is aligned with the energy of pure survival instinct that is innate in all human beings. The consciousness of the second initiation was focused on sexuality and rose through the second chakra. During this transformation (over thousands of years), the male (power) and female (creativity) aspects, along with the reproduction of the human race, were being aligned. It was during the second initiation that negative forces had evolved. Choice and the Law of Karma were brought into the consciousness of humanity in an effort to transform negative influences on the human psyche.

At present, and to a great extent, humanity is passing through the third initiation. This essentially means that emotional balance of the solar plexus (the third chakra centre) and the vibration of negative forces that are connected to it (such as jealousy and fear) are being transformed. These forces seek to keep your awareness of the differences between higher and lower consciousness-orientation separated. Harmony between these opposing poles would spell disaster for the ego's identity. The force of the lower nature I term "ego", and some of the tools that the ego uses are fear, judgement, jealousy, lies, expectations, dramas, victimhood and not being present. The activation of these energies keeps you and everyone else in the dark. It is in these areas that many of humanity's troubles arise. Much of the darkness we find in our societies rises out of ignorance of logic, ego dominance and the emotional responses therein.

Chapter 3

Understanding the Emotional Body

The emotional body is an energy field that is a prime motivating factor in the lives of many people today. This is caused by the facts that:

1: The emotional body is where the bulk of human beings centre their consciousness.

2: It is the most developed of bodies in most people at this time and receives the bulk of the life energy from the soul.

3: It knows its purpose and is able to express itself through physical experience.

4: In the minds of the lower-thinking person, it is fixed on desires and the needs of the physical. The emotional body will strongly protect and defend its interests.

5: In the initiating disciple, the emotional body turns its head up and away from the logical towards soul consciousness. This is when the process is no longer downward looking, but the energies concerned seek to rise upward instead (into the higher mind) and awakening has occurred.

6: The emotional body of the human being is the latest body of energy to be developed after the development and transformation of the root chakra (basic survival, sacral chakra (reproduction and sexuality, male female) has been largely addressed. The etheric and the physical bodies were the first two bodies of energy to be created in the order of time. The emotional body is strong, alive and powerful in most people. It reached a high point in late Atlantean times (some 50,000 years ago) and its potency is still being felt throughout the various cultures of today. The emotional body is an energy field which has a great effect upon the mass of people today. When this force is combined with the energies of the sexual centre, it can become fixed upon the emotional body as a further point of expression. Approximately half of human disease arises from emotional imbalance.

I wish to remind you here that the term "emotional body" is slightly misleading. It gives the idea that the emotional body has a specific shape or form. The emotional body is a mixture of forces (metaphysical) working through the consciousness in the form of desire, impulses, longings, wishes, determinations, incentives and projections. Much of modern psychology is based on understanding these forces. The emotional centre and the power it holds are slowly diminishing due to the greater intervention of higher consciousness (4D). This I term the "third initiation", which is changing the way in which people manage their emotions - to not be lost in them, but to be true to the self. By transforming the controlling issues of the emotional body and its power, it will no longer be recognised or used in the initiate's daily living. This is where the experiences of life transformation can be used to help others. If not, one may remain caught up in the dramas of life or see oneself as a victim of circumstance. This is when experience – the greatest teacher of life – becomes wisdom.

When the emotional body is overactive it can have a great impact upon the etheric body, often felt as emotional turmoil, which can produce great solar plexus difficulties due to the energies and forces that meet in the emotional body. This is where various conflicts arise such as anger and jealousy; it is also where the ego can make its mark by flooding the logical mind with emotional thoughts in an attempt to control the consciousness therein. Humanity in general is currently facing great challenges as attempts are made to understand emotional responses, in order for transformation to take place. When accomplished by the individual, greater balance and harmony will occur in their life principle.

The emotional body is also strongly affected by the Moon and its cycles. The full Moon and new Moon can have a strong influence, especially for those whose lives are based in solar plexus energy. If the emotional body is over stimulated it can also influence the nature of desire, be it sexual or materialistic. These two combined energies – sexual and emotional – create a great force that is often difficult for the individual to control. This in part can be due to the natural vibration or forces of the Moon, as it was once a major planet of expression.

The emotional body is a great reflector and receiver of energies. It takes in all vibration, sounds and movement from the surrounding environment that it finds itself in.

- It receives the imprints of every passing desire.
- It makes contact with every whim and fancy that is in its near environment.
- Every current (thought) sets it in motion.
- Every sound causes it to vibrate.

The emotional body is also closely aligned with the *physical willpower and its logical master.* The over stimulation and use of physical willpower drains the body of its energy, which can have a strong negative effect upon the etheric body. The etheric body is the blueprint of the physical body and it is electromagnetic in its nature. It surrounds the physical body and stands between seven and twelve centimetres from it. This is often felt as a freezing of the flow of energy (chi). Emotional fear is an energy which devitalises the etheric body. If, for example, an individual continues to use *physical willpower* to manifest their goals or life principles over a long period of time (weeks or months), the effects can be very damaging to the central nervous system and certain organs, such as the liver and kidneys. It is often the case that illnesses arise from the over stimulation of this centre, some of which are mental (depression, strong nervous tension), and addictions to alcohol and narcotics or stomach troubles and cancer, which are examples of the effects of a strong emotional imbalance.

It is possible for you to learn how to inhibit all negative forces by beginning to train your emotional body to receive and register only those impressions which come from your feelings and the intuitive or the higher self.

A method to transform negative emotions

Let's say that you are confronted by an angry person. In this instance, as in others hereafter, you should visualise your emotional body not as a sponge (which absorbs and holds all energies), but as a filter. The filter gathers the important bits of information it receives from the angry person (what they may be accusing you of). The angry person may be blaming you for something which was not your doing.

When you feel that you have gathered the relevant information, hold them for a few brief moments. Do not attack the person with what you are now holding (feelings etc), but instead imagine that in front of you there is a lift. As the door opens, step into the lift with the information you hold. Press the green button. The lift will rise up into your higher consciousness (4D) and stop. When the door opens, step out into a soft light energy.

Here you are far away from the control and responses of your emotional self and ego. You can now look for solutions or ideas as to why the person is angry with you. Don't view it as being personal; you are free from its drama and emotional responses. Look for solutions from 4D consciousness. From there you can bring the energy down into the third eye chakra. This will give you an opportunity to see what is occurring through spiritual insight; it may add pictures to your thoughts. Then bring the energy down into the throat chakra where you will hear what is being said to you on a different level. It is no longer emotional but has greater clarity. Your response will contain words of wisdom, not of judgement or attack. From there you bring the energy down into the heart chakra where the feeling will be of acceptance and love, rather than sending anger back towards the person who is angry towards you.

The last step is to bring the energy down from higher consciousness activity into your solar plexus, where your emotional body resides. At this point very little of the old original energy will be left and your response to the person attacking you will have changed into one of understanding and compassion. In this manner, you do not feed the one attacking you with a negative response. The situation will have changed, and that may produce a better outcome because the ego sees itself in the mirror of your response. Then the outer darkness can be transformed from within because you have asked for greater understanding to come on some level – call it divine insight. This is a passive, non-violent method of communication that will eventually make the necessary changes we all seek from within ourselves. It must be practiced from within; this is what Mahatma Gandhi taught.

In the method above, you are essentially stepping out of 3D into 4D consciousness. It is good practice to continually ask yourself, "Which level of consciousness am I now present in - 3 or 4D?" Point of notice! This approach may at times cause a stronger reaction from the person confronting you. If so, then you know that you have pressed the right button, whereby possible positive change can take place. It is wise to remember that you are not responsible for how any individual responds to you. Your part is to present your truth as clearly as possible without fear.

Through developing awareness in this manner, that the controlling powers of the emotional body will gradually become less and less present, as they must eventually obey the higher forces of your consciousness. The aim is to make it reflect back to you (the feeler) only that which is of the physical body (your emotional energy) and not to take anything personally. This will bring peace and harmony into your emotional and physical bodies. When this form of consciousness (non-personal) is lived by and worked on, you live and move through a positive force. You are not just blowing in the winds of thought, to rise in the tide of emotional desires, needs and fear.

What words should describe the emotional body?

Still, serene, unruffled and quiet, at rest or of a mirror-like quality, the surface of which is like a clear watery reflector that does not hold onto any feeling longer than is necessary.

When emotional energy has been transformed, it becomes a centre that accurately transmits the wishes and aims of the higher self and not the controlling needs of the lower personality.

How shall the emotional body be balanced?

It is clear from the above that in order to master the emotional body, one must fully understand its forces and powers. By studying and making positive choices in regards to the three steps given below, you will accomplish much in this important transformational process.

1: By the constant watching of desires and the motives that often cross your horizon on a daily basis. This course of action will lead you to work with a higher order of thought – 4D consciousnesses - and not the lower mind self!

2: By a constant daily attempt to live in the present moment that will reflect your true wishes of your daily life. At first mistakes will be made until little by little the positive building process will take form. Such actions will allow you to reach up into the soul guidance that all beings seek. It is from this level of consciousness that you will find the release that is being sought by you from all negative forces deep within.

3: By making a daily practice of stilling your emotional body. Much is said of stilling the mind, but it should be remembered that the stilling of the emotional body is a step nearer to the quietening of the mental body. One succeeds the other, and it is indeed wise to begin at the bottom of the ladder of consciousness.

4: It is wise to remember that you cannot transform or heal emotions with emotions! Neither is it possible to transform fear with fear. Emotions do not have the tools or the ability to do either, which is why the ego uses emotion and fear to keep you in the dark. They keep their identity by trapping your feelings and thoughts, by creating and keeping the illusion of fear alive within you. Your guiding light can lift the control they have over you. *Transformation of the lower self can only be established through higher consciousness activity.*

Part of the process of inner development is to look at whether you find it easier to be in a positive vibration (harmony) or a negative one (disharmony). Negative vibrations can be fear, worry, personality desires of any kind, personal love of anything or anyone, discouragement, oversensitivity to public opinion, guilt and self judgement. When you look deeply at all these issues then you may seek to overcome the negative vibrations by imposing a *new rhythm upon them from within yourself.* A positive rhythm of thought will definitely eliminate those negative dark controlling forces, whilst at the same time creating and developing a constructive view of life. It is wise to remember that such an undertaking is usually gradual. This is because the higher polarisation of consciousness that you seek will at first shift from one sub-plane to another.

A good way to view this process is to imagine (visualise) that you are crossing a bridge from the 3D into 4D, and at times you slip back into the 3D. The steps are gradual but can be strong because the consciousness shift will also have an effect on your cellular memory level. This may awaken negative memories held within the cells of your physical body, which also require transformation. The experiences will be marked by certain tests and initiations that will occur night and day in your daily life. These are the first small initiations and experiences which will eventually lead to a second greater initiation, the eventual transformation of the emotions.

When transformation has been fully accomplished, the initiate stands free from any negative emotional influences, which includes other people's projections of their emotional energy that seek to influence and control them. The initiate will now be able to recognise and understand such forces as they appear, and will no longer be influenced by them. They pass by and as they do they are seen for what they are and are negated. The initiate no longer gets sucked into any form of fear. The clarity of their higher consciousness will have helped them to master their lower nature so that they stand free in their light of truth and will respond accordingly.

It must be stated that the law and energy of kundalini (energy transformation of energy consciousness along the spinal cord and chakra centres) is strongly enforced by universal consciousness. This is in an effort to help transform all aspects of psyche (including the emotional body) towards higher consciousness orientation. Kundalini[27] is the three universal fires (consciousness) of creation that enters through the crown chakra of all human beings. Kundalini energy passes down the spinal cord to awaken the root chakra. The energy then rises upwards in an effort to lift, clear and cleanse any impediments,

---

27 Kundalini is the power of life. It is one of the forces of nature that carries three fires of release and transformation through the chakras. Its powers are released and influenced by conscious activity. The effects of which are deeply connected to the spinal cord and the entire chakra system.

such as negative emotional feelings and mental control issues. Negative forces can be held within one or more chakra centres if the ego and/or emotions are controlling the life principle. All negative forces hinder and block the path of higher vibrations, those of love, light and truth.

Any form of negative thinking will attract negativity. This is why group negativity or positivity is so strong, as it contains a collective consciousness. The chemistry (physical) and the psychic (spiritual) forces that underpin the consciousness of any human being, as well as their 4D consciousness, are required to be understood in order to help love, light and joy to be present. It is my belief that there must be a global consciousness shift from lower to higher consciousness for any real change to happen. For example, it is my belief that without the wisdom of 4D higher consciousness being implemented in our educational structure, little change will occur. Globally at present, consciousness is mainly focused on the left hemisphere, that of duality, mechanistic logic, achieving and competing, the qualities of the ego and the mechanistic approach. This is why the logic and emotional aspects continue to struggle to liberate themselves from the control that the lower nature imposes upon itself through society's behavioural patterns.

The lower self does not know or recognise that it is trying to liberate itself from itself!

This is clearly seen by studying the behaviour pattern of human nature. Those that continue to fight each other mainly seek the answers from outer instead of inner recognition. The human race continues to fulfil its needs (emotionally based) by over indulging, be it through over eating or having greater materiality. How much longer will this continue to keep the human psyche in the shadow of its own doing? If you look at how the ego demonstrates it's will through achieving, to have more and more of the same things, to be better than the other; you may then recognise that each experience is trying to demonstrate where you are on your path of awakening. Have you woken up yet? Has the light been switched on in a room within you to demonstrate where your resistance to change may be? With each choice you make there comes inertia, cause and effect, action and reaction. You are trying to find a way through the clouds of darkness to make sense to the life you are living by being in the light. The greatest choice you have made so far is perhaps to say no to your fears, and now you are trying to work out why.

The term "to suffer" or "suffering" are common terms that many use to justify difficult times. But this much used word "suffer" is also part of the illusion that the ego has created. Let me turn it around by saying that there is no such thing as suffering, it is a total illusion! You are having an experience instead! The experience only becomes suffering if you take what is happening to you personally.

Let me put it another way. There is no such thing as an accident and nothing happens by chance. Words commonly used by logic to justify something are "chance" and "accident". Everyone attracts to themselves what is true to the universal flow. Experiences are a means by which the individual soul can grow so long as the experience is not taken personally. If you have greater understanding of spiritual values (have woken up) you may be already taking the next step by deciding to stay out of the dramas of life and no longer feel like a victim in order to liberate your lower self from your ego. On such a journey it is important to ask yourself,

"What is the message behind the experience?" If you use this as a "mantra" (repeating it to yourself with certain experiences) it will help and encourage you to find different solutions within yourself. This can also happen if you simply allow the experience to be what it is by accepting it rather than trying to change it to suit your preconditioned mind. The opposite is to blame and judge yourself or another! Through acceptance, not judging, you will become more grateful for all experiences instead of looking for blame or fault in the self or another. These are but a few ways to help you transform negative thinking. In this manner you will take positive steps to transform the dark side whenever you activate such light consciousness.

Evil is a master of deception, and has many forms that can rise and change into something that can become much greater, and anger is such a force. The vibration of evil and darkness is held closest to the earth in what I call the "underworld". The underworld is not, as the word may suggest, directly in the earth itself, but is seen esoterically as a band of energy that encircles the earth, just outside its atmosphere. There are ancient teachings that tell us, that when a soul is departing the physical body it must first pass through the darkness to reach the light. Tibetan Buddhism, for example, goes into detail of such a transition in order that the soul may find the correct path home. I have personally entered this dark belt as a means of service and in an effort to help transform some forms of darkness that reside within its vibration.

Ways in which evil seeks to control your life force
Evil tries to master life chiefly through dominating levels of consciousness, feelings and emotion. Let us look more deeply into these levels.

The lower mind: this area holds the least resistance to dark forces. This is due to the fact that the logical aspect finds it very difficult to be fully present at any given moment, particularly if the individual lives an ego based life. When you are lost in the past or future, you cannot be present, your consciousness is then focused on fear and control and not the "absolute". When not present you are not standing in the light, your soul vibration. This leaves room for other thoughts to persist, which awaken the ego's response to the life principles that the individual holds. From there the consciousness can deteriorate into negative thinking. A fearful thought is one of the strongest controlling factors that must be mastered. Fear is a seedbed in which negativity and evil can germinate. It is also true to say that negative dark forces can pass on to other people, simply by thinking of them in a negative way; your thoughts are that powerful. However, the opposite is also true - your thoughts of love and light. The universal laws follow the same path for darkness as for light, the only difference being the intention behind the thought or feeling. This is what activates its force and powers. Your positive thought draws your consciousness towards higher-consciousness orientation, which is the consciousness of relativity.

Whenever you are being present you are tapping into the forces of relativity, but to have a balanced consciousness it is required to have a proportionate perception of life. To balance logic (absolute) and spiritual (relative) is a positive way forward.

Feelings: everyone has feelings. To listen to your feelings is of great importance because feelings are transformed emotions. They speak from the heart and not from the emotions. The initial feeling is the true one because it is intuitive and is therefore seeking to take you to the light.

But how often do you listen to and act on the first feeling in any given situation? If fear is present, that fear will activate your logic or emotions, sometimes both, which will then create doubt around your first gut-feeling. Then you become lost in past or future scenarios. Darkness has managed to take you away from your power of light, clear thinking and intuitive insight. So you may ask – "Where is my trust[28] and faith?" By learning to trust your feelings you are automatically developing your faith. Faith is a feeling; it is a knowing that all is well in your world and that you can manage and hold whatever you are experiencing without being lost in it.

The emotional body: the emotional body is prone to the influence of the ego, which is chiefly connected to the identity of the lower personality. The emotional identity seeks recognition from identifying itself with one's dramas and victimhood that the lower self often creates. Whenever you feel sorry for yourself, you are either in a drama or feel like a victim, maybe both at the same time. These appear in order to try and keep you in the shadow side of your life, which often leads to your feeling that you have little energy and this can lead to depression. Emotional responses can keep you away from your spiritual[29] life force and from trusting the higher self (soul). The emotional body holds many memories, all of which have a bearing on your life. If, for example, a negative memory appears and you think about it in a wrong way, that thought and feeling will try to keep you under its influence, which could be one of fear or attack. By changing your way of thinking (negative to

28 Insight of this nature enables the individual to use their higher sense, giving insight to trust their feelings, which can then build into having faith, true knowing.

29 Spiritual life force is the active consciousness of the soul demonstrating itself through the movement of the physical body. In physical death both leave the body, making it lifeless.

positive) emotional responses are less likely to flood the mental body and new horizons will appear because you have created them.

Intuition: the dark side continually tries to block intuitive thoughts, chiefly through the mediums of fear and control. By transforming your fears you take the necessary steps into the light which will then transform the shadow's powers of illusionary fear.

The higher senses: evil continually tries to find ways in which to block the development of the three higher senses,[30] those of clairvoyance, clairaudience and clairsentience. In this way, evil seeks to prevent all light workers from working. Possession is a clear example of how a dark force has entered an individual's temple (human body) in order to have greater control over their soul's journey. What is possession? Possession is an alien energy or force that has entered the human or animal's psyche in an effort to control its thoughts, feelings and movements. There are various levels of possession, as I will explain later in Chapter 7.

Evil's purpose is to keep fear alive in the hearts of humanity in order to block faith, love and light. If given the opportunity, evil will germinate from a simple negative thought, which is why it is so important to guard against the negative thinking of another person, event or happening. A negative thought could be emotionally based, and if held in the consciousness it will continue to grow. If you hold onto negative thoughts, they will be stored within the emotional body. Negativity can be activated through anger that can flood the mind to demonstrate its power by attacking individuals through lower consciousness (3D) activity. This is when a person

---

30 There are eight senses i.e. five physical and three nonphysical that give spiritual insight.

can become an emotional thinker rather that a logical thinker. Such energy can be linked to the lower chakra's orientation that can draw out anything that is negative. The negative dark energy will then use that force by adding it to what has already been activated. This creates further deeper negativity. The logical and emotional qualities of an individual are the weakest aspect of lower personality,[31] and are the most prone to interference by dark forces. I would define darkness at this point as being connected to fear, jealousy, judgement, expectations, needs and dependencies. Separation (from spiritual soul activity) is its motto and control is its influence.

Evil never seeks to enter through the door of higher consciousness because love and light resides within and above the 4D consciousness. Evil cannot be present in any form of divine light, as this would dissolve its identity, just like the darkness goes when you light a candle in a dark room. However within 3D consciousness there lies the basic instinct of survival (survival in this context having many connotations) which is often clouded by the ego's needs. For example, if a person has a fear of physical death, there is a weakness within the psyche due to the unknown quality of life. Evil manipulates the psyche[32] of any individual through the use of fear. One way it does this is to influence the way an individual perceives the future, because the logical aspect of humans fears most what it cannot see or understand. This

---

31 There are two personality levels. The first is the lower personality which demonstrates the physical aspects of the integrity. Higher personality is the soul quality, which is the consciousness not influenced by the vibrations of the lower personality's, such as fear, judgment, jealousy or control.

32 The psyche refers to all energies that hold life together in the physical form. The human body has eight senses. The three higher senses are connected to the lower five physical senses. However at some point in time all five senses will be open and functional, then the psyche is fully functional. Intuition is one of the easiest energies to accept or recognise that is connected to ones psyche.

perception often creates doubt in the mind, which results in confusion. The confused state is a lack of being present in one's power, this often creates chaos, and chaos can lead to a general breakdown of the entire central nervous system. In this instance it may become clearer how evil can take hold of the psyche through controlling the perception of past, present and future, which are of the 3D vibration - the ego's domain.

I often refer to darkness or evil as a shadow in order to give people a mental picture of it. The shadow of the lower nature will come from behind to stand in front of you; it is there to block your path of being present and creating doubt and confusion. Whenever this happens to you, you can demand that the shadow stands behind you as you wish to move forward. When you have made that positive decision, the shadow must obey as you have empowered that thought through your light force. Whenever the term *"without a shadow of a doubt"* is used we are actually sharing a sacred law that removes doubt within the mind. Then there can be no dark area that remains hidden within.

The spoken word is one of the seven sacred breaths of creation. The spoken word is consciousness unfolding. Humanity often speaks through the lower consciousness in order to get things done on a practical physical level. It is here that much confusion and negativity can be created if the words used are manipulative. It is wise to remember that all levels of consciousness hold great powers and deserve respect, regardless of which way one chooses to express their consciousness through the spoken word.

There is no truer saying than, *"Evil is what you make it out to be."* Evil, dark spirits, ghouls, poltergeists and masters of darkness are realities that will only hold true for you for as long as you believe in and fear them. These are energies that are food for evil; they feed its endless needs! In fact fear is at the heart of all that is dark and evil; as are judgement and jealousy, as they continually seek to separate you from your power of truth and light! The vibration of fear can only resonate within 3D consciousness, which has both weakness and strength, depending on its use and the motivation that is behind it.

There are three types of fear

1: *Natural fear,* this may make you run away faster from some form of danger or it may freeze you. I call this "instinctive fear" and it is deeply held in the psyche.

2: *Mental fear,* which is often created by being told to fear something or someone. Children and adults alike are conditioned in such ways. The media is apt at creating fear.

3: *Emotional fear,* this fear can rise out of a past negative feeling that has not been healed or transformed. A fear may arise due to the belief that such a happening will occur in the same way, which is connected to past and future fears.

The more advanced states of evil that have possessed an individual are able to read their energy and thoughts; you could call this a "psychic interpretation". It therefore stands that the intelligent dark force has insight into anyone's weaknesses. It can read your aura, see into your etheric body and interpret your chakra centres in seconds. It sees the colours that you are attracting into your aura through your consciousness activity and as such is able to read your thoughts. Negative energy will follow the line of energy to see where your fear may be. This is in part how evil chooses where it wishes to be, which could be in a dwelling, as in haunted house or another individual human being. Its environment is very important to it, just as it is for you! The saying "like attracts like" is a law that often applies to evil. Evil gathers those with similar intent, which could be within the premises of another being's consciousness. The underworld[33] is full of macabre dwellings, towns and places that are truly holographic. I know of this as I have entered such places to do some deep rescue work.

Evil is predominantly about control over goodness, light and love - it's opposite. Here laws of duality come into full play. For how would you know the difference between goodness and evil if you had not experienced them? Levels of control are present in all four lower kingdoms – mineral, plant, animal and human. All kingdoms to a greater or lesser degree are corrupted by some form of darkness, through humanity's doing. This is not a new phenomenon. The battle between the two opposing forces of evil and love, darkness and light is aeons old. It will only end when all forms of evil have been transformed from the face of the earth, which requires the old consciousness to be transformed into a collective harmonious flow of universal light. All energy forms that emanate from the original evil "dark brotherhood" are illusions that have been created through the mind's ability to fear and are therefore of the mind. There has been a battle raging between these two opposing forces for millennia.

An important part of transforming the darkness that I speak of here is to look beyond what you literally see and

33 This is a dark belt of energy that lies just outside of the earth's aura. It is where all dark and evil forces collect because they are unwilling to return to the light for further spiritual transformation. They choose not to reincarnate under the law of karma to transform any negative forces.

feel through the physical eyes. The eyes can fool you because they are controlled by the lower mind. Yes, it is not the eyes that see - it is the mind. In order to be realised, to go beyond fear of darkness, look beyond the horizon of how your physical eyes control your perceptions of life. Strive with every breath to develop your higher sense though higher mind orientation. Then the spiritual eye, your third eye,[34] will begin its development as a natural way towards your own enlightenment. Then you will be given the tools to see the dark forces as well as light forces, and fear will transcend into faith.

The illusion of evil can manifest itself by dropping its vibration into 3D consciousness in order for you to see it on a physical level. One example I have experienced is seeing writing on a mirror in a house that was possessed by a poltergeist.

It is important to state here that not all dark forces or ghosts are necessarily evil, or appear to do harm. A common benign ghost may simply drop its vibration, to show itself in order to be seen. Ghosts of this nature are normally trapped between two realms[35] and require assistance in order to continue their journey by returning to heaven. I have also had experience of strong dark forces appearing before me to be transformed. With this understanding it is important to take each experience individually and act accordingly; otherwise an opportunity to transform a dark force may be missed, purely in the belief that it is going to do you or others harm, and this is not necessarily true.

The poltergeist does things in order to tap into your psyche by awakening your fear. Evil looks to feed itself

---

34 The higher vibration of light that stimulates the third eye exceeds the physical light under which the physical eyes views life.

35 Heaven and earth.

off your fears. It could be said that all evil is a vampire that takes our energy and power away. It does this in a variety of ways, such as through fear and judgement. This is how it seeks to take control of the life force, the soul's vibration. This is the ultimate aim of any evil that seeks to possess another, *When a shadow falls upon the Soul.*

Chapter 4

From First to Third Initiation

In the first initiation the first or root chakra was fully functional in all human beings. Its purpose was to implant the basic instincts of survival in the consciousness. Now the principle of the first initiation is deeply embedded in the psyche of all humans. Such an instinct can appear in a flash that may even save your life, it is innate. The consciousness then rose from the base chakra through into the second chakra, which was where the second initiation took place.

In the second initiation: the consciousness was activated towards the sexual and reproduction process. More souls were required to fulfil the greater universal plan,[36] which has led humanity to a critical crossroads which is being witnessed and experienced on the evolutionary path of people today. In many of today's societies, sexuality is still a major driving force that is has extended itself more towards outer appearances than inner sacredness of sexuality. Until this trend is reversed, the ego will continue to control much of what occurs at present, through second chakra stimulation.

The third initiation: humanity is presently working with and passing through a most critical period of self-

---

36 Souls demonstrate through the physical experiences how darkness and evil traps and controls through actions and reactions of violence and revenge. The great plan is to break this hold through spiritually awakening every soul on earth, i.e. raising consciousness.

transformation. I call this period the "third initiation". It chiefly concerns the transformation of the lower personality which is logic, emotional body and the ego-self. The life experiences that each individual attracts are helping to enlighten their 3D consciousness towards 4D awareness.[37] For this to occur there must be an effort by all humans to awaken their soul's consciousness.[38] This can be accomplished by turning on the light within those rooms of your temple (the physical self). The switch is already there. By opening your higher mind, greater light (wisdom) can be passed into the logical room of thought. Then you may begin to see where there are shadows, such as negative thought. Or there may be anger stored in the room of your emotions. Prior to the room receiving more light you may have thought that everything was fine, and that all was well in your world. But when the light is switched on, the ego will be seen for what it truly is. You will then begin to understand how it has been keeping you in the dark as you see your past dramas, your victimhood and future fears in another light. This, the third initiation, requires your permission to open your mind towards esoteric science, which will eventually open the door to your higher consciousness and senses therein. This will eventually deliver you to your awakening of super consciousness - your 5D consciousness and beyond.

As a point of reference, I call 3D lower and 4D higher consciousnesses personalities. But what is the lower personality? A personality is an identity label that basically illustrates a person's persona; some would call it the "I." Every person has a psyche and an awareness of their physical body as well as a subtle awareness of their spirit

37 Energy awareness. A realisation on a deeper level of what energy is and how it impacts everyone's lives.

38 The divine forces of love, joy and peace.

and soul bodies. Within the psyche, all energy forms are at work, the majority are metaphysical, the likes of which are the aura, etheric body and chakras. Others are your feelings, emotions, temperament of mind, love, joy and peace. These energies provide each person with experience of physical life through the five senses and the three spiritually-orientated senses. The first five senses are governed by physical laws, giving meaning and direction therein. The senses of smell, touch, taste, hearing and sight are well developed within the human psyche. It is in this area that we find one of the strongest human vibrations, that of survival. On the physical plane there can be a weak point where a negative force (evil) may try to dominate the life force of an individual by creating fear. The three higher senses, those of clairvoyance, clairaudience and clairsentience give insight to an advanced soul, such as a healer or medium, to make contact with all spiritual forces, such as the light energy of spirit guides, as well as the dark force of a poltergeist. Then the individual will be able to meet all spirit forms on all levels. The spiritually developed individual can then apply their healing gifts (spiritual hands on healing or thought projection) towards transforming what is negative; in this manner they are serving the greater good.

The dark force knows that there is no escape from the all seeing light; there is no hiding place in the universe from such an advanced light being. The transformation of the dark force will be completed when applied correctly by a master of light.

Humanity on the whole is currently passing through the third initiation - regardless of whether they are conscious of it or not. The transformation of one's ego, fears, expectations, needs and logical control factors are key areas that are now being addressed from a higher-mind principle. The vibrations of the lower mind and ego-self are the chief dominating force that is blocking, or at the very least, seeking ways to impair, the transformational process from 3D rising into 4D consciousness. The forces of lower consciousness are locked into the dense physical senses to help give perspective to physical experiences, but they can also recreate the illusions that fear manifests. Fear continually seeks to dominate the physical psyche through the choices one makes and the action or reactions that follow. The lower personality (ego) requires its identity to be seen and recognised in all aspects of life. These rise out of the lower plane of consciousness like a wave in the ocean that seeks the shore. The emotional body and its responses - right down to its identity - are prime factors that must be mastered in order to transform 3D consciousness.

Do you feel that you are entering higher consciousness and the third initiation of spiritual development? One sure sign is that you begin to question your own set of values, such as judgements or doubts. Another is that you begin to feel dismayed about your life because you feel empty, not fulfilled, even when you have achieved something on the material level. As you start to question your core values you may have a feeling that there is no going back, the drive to move onwards and upwards is too great. Identity change then occurs as the lower personality loses control over its physical apparatus and the higher consciousness seeks deeper meanings to truth and peace.

A key word to consider here is "control". Ask yourself this basic question: what control issues do you have in your life at present and why do you have them? For example: when you hear someone, your boss perhaps, say that they need to make people feel guilty to get them motivated, to do better than they have tried to do, what are your thoughts about this? This is an egotistical abuse of power. Such a person is basically playing with people's emotions and this is a negative game that has a dark side. Making the person feel that they are not worthy can touch upon a fear that lies deep in the heart and body of the individual. This is a misuse of consciousness. There are mental and emotional dark forces that are often used by those who hold deep fear in themselves. An individual making another feel guilty is the mirror effect of fear attracting fear. For example, the sender of fear may be fearful of losing something but this case does not believe that the emotion will come back to him/her. This is why the attacker always sends the message away from themselves. In this situation guilt is secondary; fear is the prime motivator, even though it is unconscious.

Whenever anyone's control is mentally-based, it is more dangerous than emotionally-based control. Mental control can often be cold and calculating. Emotionally-based control often succumbs to its own emotional responses and will collapse under its own impulses or pressure. The true and often hidden force behind any form of control is fear. You may now begin to see more clearly how the ego is connected to fear (often through the emotions) as a means of controlling its own environment, which can include other people. The physical body can bring you neither peace nor turmoil, neither joy nor pain. It is a means, and not an end, to life itself. The physical body has no purpose by itself, only to what is given to it, in other words, your thoughts, emotions and feelings. Guilt and fear are both conditions of the mind to be obtained. And these conditions are the home of the emotion that calls them forth and therefore becomes compatible with them. But ask yourself which is it that is compatible with you: guilt, fear or peace?

Everything (material and non material) is connected in one form or another to the creator's universal consciousness, God. This is a fact that is of great importance for all to recognise. Everyone is being touched by God consciousness, i.e. light. God is not an identity to which one holds onto in the belief that your God is your truth, the truth is in your heart where God rests.

There is no right or wrong, the experiences you have demonstrate the values you hold. You have drawn those experiences towards you in an effort to perceive your oneness with all things; this is where you will find the meaning in God. God is not in a singular thing or person, God is in all things at all times. If the butterfly flaps its wings in Australia, you will feel its vibration wherever you may be in the world. Likewise, all of our senses, thoughts and energies are connected to the collective consciousness of the world and universal consciousness, Godliness. This force is sometimes referred to as "oneness". All human beings are wired up to universal consciousness because the human being is a living body of universal energy. You and I, individually and collectively, are a universe within a universe. The human form is like the cells in the universal body of life. Each cell is a body of energy that collectively makes up the body of the universe through the consciousness held within each cell. The universe is a matrix, a numerically coded structure that is created through our thoughts. It continues to expand because individuals choose or decide what to experience. This is what has collectively created the world you live in and what is to come from our lines of thought.

The universe is a multidimensional body of energy that holds infinite possibilities. It could be said that we are a matrix within a matrix; this is how I see the reality of our creation in the created universe. Unimaginable explorations lay before humanity, but for this to truly flourish humanity must learn to truly communicate with each other through mutual respect in order to awaken those possibilities. But as you observe the world's level of consciousness that is dominant, you may realise that the human being has as yet not fulfilled even one of the basic universal laws, the law of unconditional love. *Humanity has not yet learned to get on with one another - as Christ said, "Love thy neighbour".* Without this principle truly being brought to life, there will remain separation. By embracing each other, not separating; loving not hating; accepting not judging - true harmony and joy will follow. The ego and the darkness it contains continually try to control the human psyche by helping you to forget. An obvious example of how this has impregnated and continues to manipulate the consciousness of many is in how much time is spent focusing on the negative!

The Aquarian age is upon us. These are times for greater openness; sharing and mutual respect to flourish, but it must of course start within you, me and all other beings. Princess Diana was once asked, "Why do you share so much love with everyone?"

Her answer was simple but powerful: "Someone has to."

This begs another question: "Where does anything start?" The answer is - within you, by remembering that you are a divine source of light, truth, love and joy.

Chapter 5

The Misconceptions of Fear and Hope

The concepts of these much-used words "fear and hope" are deeply engraved in the lower consciousness of individuals (the third dimensional thinker). I would even say that the lower mind is conditioned by modernity to believe that they are an important part of our existence and experience. In doing so, those who are unaware of their true identity and meaning,[39] often fall into the trap of using them to either justify something or to control a situation or others. The uses of these two words (fear and hope) are often hidden (consciously or unconsciously) behind an agenda of mistrust held in the user's psyche, and as such must carry a certain element of darkness. It follows that anything that seeks to take a person away from their inner power (that of light), such as fear, is connected to some form of darkness. This does not necessarily mean that the person is dark; but rather that they may be unaware that they are actually carrying an element of darkness by being fearful or giving fear to another. For example, negative thought is a form of darkness; it is an energy form that needs to be fed by other energies. Control is one such energy that feeds the ego and darkness connected to it, whereas light is expansive and releases.

The concepts of fear and hope are also deeply rooted in our cultural belief systems, and as such can be associated

39 One's of acceptance, love, joy and peace.

with humanity's control issues. Fear and hope are only held in the perception of third dimensional consciousness (3D) that holds strong beliefs or probabilities of past, present and future. But for now, let us focus on the past and future in order to give some deeper insights into the role that fear and hope may play in an individual's life - such as yours.

Fear is the old energy of 3D consciousness (the new being 4D consciousness) through which consciousness rising occurs. The 3D consciousness has served humanity well in the past; it is deeply connected to the natural instinct of survival. It could be said that fear is humanity's biggest controlling factor. However, I understand that fear, not instinctual fear but man-made fear, is now preventing the human race from ascending to the next level of spiritual development, that of higher consciousness transformation. The vibration of higher consciousness begins to emanate from the fourth dimension - 4D upwards. The illusions that fear creates prevent (in a variety of ways) an individual from entering and accessing their higher consciousness in order to transform fear into trust. Intuition, for example, is an aspect of your higher consciousness that is blocked by fear.

The societies we live in become more dependent upon gizmos or electrical appliances that on the outside seem to take care of things. However the downside of this is that the human intuitive quality is declining, as is the deeper sense of self-trust. For example the cell phone is often used in this way, when we are five minutes late we often call or are called to say, "I am on my way" or "I am at a certain place, I will be with you soon". Why do we do this? For me it is because we do not trust the self enough to say to the self that everything is OK, or indeed that the universe is taking care of things. Or on a deeper level try to feel where that person may be on their journey - psychically tune in to that person and you may be surprised at what comes back to you.

So what is fear? Let me give you an example of how it is used in many life situations by those who wish to control you or the masses with fear. The one seeking to control will first give or present you with the fear - for example that there is a planet heading towards earth that is going to smash into us, creating an Armageddon. Then in the second breath, that person will offer you hope by saying, "Buy my book, it offers you the only hope by which you can avoid annihilation". Is this darkness at work?

My own understanding of fear is that it is the conditioning of the lower mind that is seeking to control you by making you believe that your fears are real; the fearful thought creates or empowers the fear itself. In this respect the fearful thought goes before you, which is how most people continue to re-manifest their fears - by believing in them. This is a very deep form of conditioning that is commonly used, often to control societies, which for me *is* a dark force! The human being has been taught to believe that the illusions of all illusions (fear) is true! This is partly due to the fact that fear often stirs up emotional energy. It achieves this chiefly through a person's thought patterns by making those emotions seem much bigger than they actually are! Up to ninety per cent of average logical thoughts are emotionally based. One feeds the other. In other words, an imbalanced emotional body can and does escalate the illusions of fear. Fear often freezes one's energies and, if it does, the energy of fear can be split into two connected flows of energy.

This is how it works: if you as an individual allow your original thought (that is orientated in 3D consciousness) to enter the unbalanced emotional self, a fear may arise which can then become emotionally orientated rather than mentally processed. If the emotional energy establishes itself, then the individual can become an emotional thinker. The person giving you fear or trying to make you fearful knows this (consciously or unconsciously). It is often found that when the energy of fear reaches a certain point, such as deep frustration, it can become anger based, which is often related to a past experience. This for me is a form of ego protectionism. The ego does not want to lose its identity and will do absolutely anything to keep it! This is why fear always looks outside itself for answers; it requires feeding! It does not want to be present at any cost, it can't be! It would have no identity, being present does not require identity, it is simply being.

It is evident that all fears are based on past events or happenings (some of which may not be of this lifetime) and your experience of them determines their depth or the hold they have over you. From my experience of giving therapy, I believe that human beings often carry past life fears into this lifetime in order to transform them. This is where understanding of a karmic link can be of great help during therapy, as in why does a person keep on recreating or repeating experiences that are negative? It is my belief and experience that as a person works to transform fears within themselves, the transformation of fears will eventually take them into a greater sense of love, one of universal trust, which is a greater sense of faith. This is due to the fact that love is a higher vibration than that of fear or hope. Therefore fear and hope cannot reside in the body or mind of any individual that decides to be present in the light of the love vibration. The shadow of fear cannot be present where love is because the light dismantles or transcends the identity that fear holds, and the controlling factor is then negated.

To transform your fears, it is important to first recognise and face your inner fears. This is partly done by transforming your perception of what a past experience may be telling you in order for you to be present. It is important to learn to be present in all that you do. Whenever you are present you are in the vibration of acceptance, then it is possible to enter the vibration of forgiveness. Acceptance is a key that will open the door to forgiveness, and help to transform old thoughts and feelings.

If you are not truly present, then where are you? If you ask yourself at any given moment, "Where am I now - in the past or future?" you may find yourself in both at the same time. If so then you cannot be grounded in the present. Whenever you are not fully present you do not experience life to its fullest, the ego is active and you are being influenced by it. Yes, the ego is the seedbed of fear and hope. It is true to say that you cannot heal or transform fear with fear or emotions with emotions because they are of a similar vibration, that of 3D consciousness. Fear and love cannot co-exist; make your choice or decision, where do you want to be in any given moment? By gradually replacing your fears with a greater sense of faith, you will naturally have a deeper connection to the higher-self; you will enter a vibration of trusting yourself. When you accomplish this you will find that you will also trust others more. The development of your inner trust will take you into a higher vibration of inner-faith. Faith is a knowing - call it intuition!

Because the ego identifies itself with either the past or the future at any given moment, it cannot and does not want to be in the present moment. The ego cannot accept being present. If it did it would be out of a job! This is why, in part, logic is always so busy in wanting to achieve things. The ego wants more of this or that, to make it better than this or that. There is little light carried in such thoughts, and the shadow remains. But what happens when those needs have been fulfilled, what then? Do you want more of it? The ego's presence is strong in our society, which can be seen by how much individuals are driven by achieving rather than taking care of the self, and to be present with the self, to be still. There is much that can be achieved by simply doing nothing. Maybe this concept will stop your mind for a moment or two?

The ego is continually analysing and forming judgements of itself and others, this is an important part of the ego's self recognition and justification process. Judgement is not a universal law; it is the ego's way of justifying itself, it creates separation, which is a form of darkness. The ego says to itself, "I like this, I don't like that." This is the ego's way of giving itself energy and self recognition, which in turn can create fear. Fear is one of the ego's life forces, just as emotion is, which keeps on feeding it. This old consciousness, the energy of judgement, served the human evolution well until the universal consciousness entered the Aquarian age of higher communication.

Have you experienced how the old consciousness is no longer truly serving you or humanity? Human beings are killing each other through their judgement of each other. Examples of this can be found in such beliefs that this religion is better than that one, or you are wrong, I am right! This is the ego playing games with you; the old consciousness in a negative manner continues to separate. Whenever and wherever this occurs, evil is ruling.

Any fear you may have also creates separation by overpowering your trust and faith in yourself. Fear continually seeks to control your perception of the future, sometimes at a cost to others or even the self, which is partly why fear and ego are fascinated with the future. It is at this point that "hope" comes into the picture. Hope is not a universal word that guides or enlightens; it is a word of fear. You are giving away your power whenever you hope for something because you do not trust yourself or stay in your creative power - therefore you fear. The word "hope" is often used as a means to try and justify the future, if for example you say to someone, "I hope it will all work out well for you?" For me there is always a question mark to be added after such a statement because no one knows what the future may actually bring. So why hope for it? When hear someone give a message of hope to someone who is leaving their home by saying to them, "I hope your journey will be a good one," I am always left with an inner question of *Do they know something that I don't?* For me it is a negative projection that "something negative may happen" and the person that you have given it to will feel your own insecurity on some level.

Much if not all of the insurance industry is built upon fear, past happenings and probabilities. The stock market is based upon future speculation, the unknown. But neither of these is actually in the present. So what value do they have other than material gain? Is society protecting itself on probabilities, and even greater illusions? It seems to be that way! So what are certainties? Whenever you do not trust yourself you step out of your inner-faith and into the illusion of hope in the belief that somehow it will be fixed by someone else. Essentially you distrust yourself and as such you are giving your power away to hoping for something better. This is what others are doing to you when they give you the message of hope. Hope is a low vibration of consciousness which has created the illusions that hoping brings. This is because the ego wants you to stay in that state of lower-mind orientation, i.e. to distrust the universe and the self, which is emotional confusion brought about by fear and control issues.

Ask yourself, how many times you have told another person that you "hope they will do something about it?" Can you see how this puts them on the spot? Is it not about your own expectations of the other person, simply because you do not trust yourself?

How many times have you told someone that you hope that this or that will turn out well? This for me is again an example of a lack of trust. Underneath all of this fear there is a great force trying to tell you to get up and do something about it, rather than giving your power away to hope and fear. In this context, I believe it is wise to understand that your consciousness (regardless of which level) goes before you. This is a basic understanding of universal laws. If you have fear, you will attract it to you because you have sent out that message. It then appears in order to give you an opportunity to transform it; which is a gift, not a negative happening. This is spiritual development, viewing all experiences as opportunities, as gifts. To turn on the light in the room where you may have a fear is to see where the problem may be. You may not have even realised that you had a problem until the light was put on. Whenever this is done, a big step towards releasing the ego has occurred.

Light transforms darkness, not the other way around.

- Fear and hope are the tools of the lower self, which seeks to keep your psyche in darkness.

- There is no cosmic need to fear and hope for anything. They are the jail masters of the soul.

- Whenever you are in fear, you are not in the love vibration.

- Whenever you hope for something, you are not present in trusting the higher self or the universe's greater plan for you and those around you.

Through your spiritual development, you will step into and maintain your awareness of the higher vibration of your 4D consciousness. By activating your higher consciousness, the fears and hopes that you carry will be transformed along with the darkness they contain. This is part of the greater plan of universal consciousness transformation - clearing out of the old consciousness which no longer serves humanity. By transforming your fears and removing the word "hope" from your vocabulary and thoughts, you will have taken great steps towards self-enlightenment. These are steps to free you from the ego's control! You will feel lighter within.

The dualities of evil, darkness and pain

- You are like children in a room that is lit, whose eyes are closed, saying that you are afraid of the dark, when in fact darkness is but a disturbance of the light.

- You can understand the nature of darkness by overcoming your fears.

- Those fears are the illusions that darkness creates in order to take you away from your truth and light that you are holding within you.

- From experiencing and learning of the ways of fear you will know how it has limited your life.

- You are a being of light that often gets lost through the confusion of wrong thinking and emotional imbalance.

- You are learning.

- You are discovering who you are.

- You are altering a ten thousand year old belief system that you were brought up to believe in.

- The physical world as you have known it to be is now changing beyond recognition; the belief in darkness, the belief in the power of fear, the belief that anger has a force that can stand against love, you will understand is not true. They are illusions!

All of these are part of the experiences being manifested here on earth for the human race to learn from to step back into the light. But it was the human being that created them. In the beliefs of such things, humanity continues to re-create them, and will continue to do so until the inner-work is done to transform such beliefs in darkness.

The interesting thing is that humanity in general has not created such illusions in order to be defeated by them, but rather to learn from them through the cycle of human evolution. How else can the lower consciousness expand to rise into higher consciousness activity?

Nothing exists in the human world that is not Godly. The earth is the oneness of God's love. There is an undivided reality that embraces the dualistic world that is truly governed by love. I call this light and truth.

Evil is an ignorance of divine will and divine law. No one would resist God's guidance if they were aware that it consists of their own joys, bliss and eternal love.

If people would but realise what they do unto others they do to themselves. There is no separation from the truth of life.

Every thought is a seed ready to be cultivated. Every action or reaction is an opening of that seed.

Negative energies are indeed present in the physical world, but they have been doing God's work. Without them you would not have been offered a choice between darkness and light, and the growth process of mankind would have been hindered.

Dualities such as darkness and light have been necessary ingredients for spiritual growth. These energies are not masters in themselves; they have been the servants of God's will. And through you God's will is enacted because you are an instrument of the divine. Just as the flute is for the musician, God's breath flows through you.

Humanity is now passing through the vibration of awakening the higher consciousness of the 4D. You will realise that the old consciousness that created those very dualities is now changing - because they no longer serve the greater good. When you realise this, you will no longer be separated from your love, joy and peace. The path of the ego, along with its beliefs - such as fear - will evaporate through your conscious effort to transform them.

Negativity has within it the seeds of its own destruction! Think on this.

You experience as you believe in the world in which you live. The positive and the negative are products of what you hold to be true. This duality can serve the purpose of ultimate unification (a coming together) but only if you realise that it is the purpose of the divine will, which is to go beyond what duality represents.

As long as there are people who seek the light, there will be people who have shadows that seem to follow them. When such an image can be altered and transformed, the shadow that was blocking their light will disintegrate. There will no longer be any fear and illusions to contend with. The realisation is that physical death is but a consciousness-shift from one sub-plane to another. It is the ascending path of the soul leaving the physical body when it has fulfilled its mission in that particular life.

Duality on earth has a divine purpose. You have been participating in its creation, which is where your personal reality now lies; you may live in it, but you are not trapped by it. It is not your prison, it is your school. You have been using duality to help you find unity of spirit and soul through your higher spiritual personality. Do not become lost in the duality of the lower personality, the ego. You are now rising out of the lower nature in order to develop and maintain your higher spiritual soul vibrations. The essence of soul guidance - is activated through your higher consciousness where duality no

longer has an influence over your life's journey, oneness does.

As you accept, not blindly or uncaringly, but with an
ever-deepening awareness of your circumstances involved in human experience, you reflect more and more
upon your own light that is being poured onto those
experiences, i.e. you remain more positive.

There will come a day when, regardless of what is happening in the human community that you live in, you
will see it as a blaze of light, and from that moment onwards you will be free from fear. You will have taken a
leap of faith, to see another reality in the experience of
what humans call pain; this experience will carry you
away from the thought of suffering. Pain and darkness
are extremely compelling, and the fear of them can trap
the spirit and soul, but in some way humanity has a
fascination with them. *Do you have it, if so what is it?*

You have a physical body that aches and sometimes
screams out for help. You have emotions that seem to
tear you apart as you seek to fulfil your needs and the
fears that accompany them. In those times of stress,
ask yourself, who is it that is experiencing this? Meditate upon what disturbs you. Go beyond the physical
thought-related pain; from there you may see another
reality, such as: *Stress is unfulfilled peace!*

*The one who is aware of the experience, but is not lost in it,
is the bearer of light.*

It is from such a place of stillness, one of peace, that your
inner strength can be harnessed. Your psyche is aware of
all possibilities, never forget that. You will move in accordance with the divine laws that seek to transform and

harmonise any negative forces within you. The use of the sacred breath is one way to help move any pain that you may be feeling. You can use the breath as a spiritual force to help lift any blockage that may be there, by directing it towards your pain. Every breath you take is a sacred one and such a breath can be used to help transform your chakras. All chakras are centres of consciousness and as such are receivers of your thoughts, which are in turn empowered by the inner breath, which is connected to your heart and to universal love.

Chapter 6

Physical Death with Insights

I feel it is important to say that it is the soul's vibration that keeps the physical body alive as well as determining when it should leave the earth plane – as in physical death. It therefore stands that there is no such thing as accidental death, there is a happening. Just as there is no such thing as an accident, there is an experience.

What occurs immediately after physical death? Let us first look into what I term "the transformation of the spirit and soul from the physical body during the death process" whereby all three energy forms (physical body, spirit and soul) return to their original sources.

The physical body

If you ask yourself, "How is our physical body made and what makes it move?" what answer comes to you? If we go deeper into these questions some interesting answers arise, not all of which can be wholly found in the logical explanation of life. Humanity has been trying to answer these questions since history began. For me, the answers are held in the understanding of what roles the spirit and soul play in relation to the universal laws and events of life lived on earth.

Weight is determined by mass, and mass is determined by density. It follows that density is governed by the force of the earth's gravitational pull, which is then measured as weight in pounds or kilograms. Body mass, weight and density are measured in this manner. The physical body has been created in a perfect body weight to height ratio, which is fixed in too many forms of sciences, such as when individuals are given chemotherapy for cancer (their body weight determines the volume of chemotherapy given).

From a metaphysical and esoteric point of view, it is the light frequency in the body that determines your mass. Mass is derived from light. The more light we attract into our consciousness, the lighter the vibrations of the mass become, which is not measured in a physical manner, but in the light vibration of the spirit that resides within the dense physical body, and the soul's responses to it. An example of this can be seen whenever you are in a positive mind set; greater light enters our bodies via the mind or consciousness. Whenever you hold positive energy you may feel that you are floating along in life. The opposite situation is when you have negative thoughts and then you feel heavy. Your self-motivation is affected and it seems harder to move along or do anything. How low or depressed anyone may become is determined by how far they are from the light. It follows that the body will feel heavier and it will therefore take more physical will power or energy to move it. Negativity is a dark force that drains the physical body of its energy source. It is a circle that many get caught up in.

One positive way to draw more light energy into the physical self is to work with a chakra balancing practice. This will essentially draw more light into the chakra centres, which can only serve to have a positive effect upon the whole body system, such as the meridians, central nervous system and blood. Meditation or chanting "om"[40] may have a similar effect upon your life force.

Light is the transformational force of love, which creates the harmony you may often feel when meditating or working with light rays when healing.

But what keeps the body mass alive? What makes the physical self move? These are fundamental questions that you should explore. If you were to go deeper into seeking knowledge and wisdom from esoteric science, the understanding of life and the values of what the spirit and soul represent in the flow of life will become more complete. Then your spiritual journey may have truly begun.

The dense physical body is but an instrument that is used by the spirit and soul to seek deeper expression of the divine, whilst present on the earth plane. The physical body is etheric matter in a crystallised form that seeks to transcend itself through the electrical impulses produced from the soul's vibration of light through the electromagnetic sphere. Physical movements are an expression of the spiritual force being directed by soul consciousness. The physical form is also a matrix of sacred numerical and geometrical form. It is an instrument of both outward and inward universal expression that is experienced on the physical plane through the common senses of smell, touch, hearing, vision and taste. The higher self - the three higher senses when awakened sufficiently - correspond to your ability to use your clairvoyance, clairaudience and clairsentience. The

40 The sacred word "om" vibrates a voice of harmony that passes through all conflicts (the conflicts being the pair of opposites) which bring forth the vibratory activity which will lead to eventual unity, harmony, right relations and to the release of intuition.

physical self is held together by electrical impulses via higher forces of metaphysical proportions.

The main purpose of the physical body is to serve others by developing and practicing spiritual values. This temporary temple helps to ground the higher vibrations of the spirit and soul through the polarisation of those forces. The atomic and sub-atomic forces of light frequencies are reduced in power to accommodate the electromagnetic field of the etheric body, which in turn connects to the central nervous system on the physical level. This inflowing energy is sometimes referred to as chi or prana, which flows in a circular movement up and down the spinal cord connecting all seven chakras. Higher consciousness is held both within the physical brain and the higher consciousness field of the aura. The consciousness of the soul can only be developed by firstly accessing it (which can be seen as putting a light on in a room of your temple) to transform the lower consciousness and the ego towards higher-consciousness orientation. When a light is put on by you, the seeker, in a room of your temple, you may begin to ask questions about life itself, or you may find something about yourself that you do not like. You may find at times that the choices you make may be difficult because they no longer serve your lower self, the ego.

Once the physical body has been created, it will mature and develop - as do the psychic forces within it. All organs such as the liver or kidneys have their own particular vibration. All bodies of energy that help make complete the physical body – as in the seven chakras - are only fully developed when you reach the age of twenty-one.

The physical body is designed and built to take the knocks and blows of everyday living. To a degree it is able to grow or rebuild some damaged parts, such as the liver and skin, but sometimes the damage it sustains can be too extreme for full recovery.

The soul enters the body of the womb during the magical moment of conception. This is a moment that unifies heaven and earth, male and female. From that moment onwards the information (DNA) from the three bodies of mother, father and the soul - light - of the child, begin to build the physical body. The physical body closely follows its previous blueprint of its last physical form. This is in order that it may build onto the physical form to improve and make well any imperfections that it may have developed during the last life span – which is partly why the parents are chosen for their DNA imprints.

When the consciousness of an individual rises, and such qualities as intuition are used, it follows that it may help to create a stronger and healthier physical form. But even with what, from a logical perspective, may seem to be an imperfect body (as in diseased or crippled), there is still spiritual growth at work. For example, a lack of mobility of the physical body may be of crucial importance from a soul level, but can be seen as a hindrance physically. The mind and emotional responses often get in the way of the deeper - spiritual - insight of a limiting physical condition. It is not for anyone to judge, but to accept that it is the path of an individual, and then ask how they can help, if needed. With this understanding, I have recognised that our body type is also a great teacher. It may have been with you in a similar form for many lifetimes. The gender may change from time to time; as each lifetime will follow in accordance to the universal soul's desire to develop. The soul is always fully present from the moment of conception. The soul is as big and complete from the moment of conception as any fully grown adult is. The spirit gradually builds itself within as the new physical body develops over the nine months of pregnancy and continues until the individual reaches the age of twenty-one. With each lifetime, the physical body is learning new skills to be used by the soul, but the soul holds the knowledge of all lifetimes that are ready to be awakened and used to serve others.

During the last month of pregnancy the soul reaches the completion of the body type and rebirth will ensue.

Both the spirit and soul are creators of the physical body. From its new temple the soul will seek to transform the forces of the lower mind and its nature through the spiritual will into a being of higher consciousness, a temple of light.

The length of time that everyone spends as a physical being is dependent upon two main factors:

1: The amount of karmic debt[41] that has been created and the development it seeks to achieve; this is determined by the soul's consciousness.

2: The new karma that is created thereafter with all that it entails.

The energy of the body mass is held together by the soul's vibration, which has the eyes to see and the consciousness to understand all things. The spirit is the will, or driving force of the soul which listens to and obeys its master. The spirit, as a form of energy, is not able to fully leave the physical body until the consciousness of the soul has completely withdrawn itself on death and the physical body begins to disintegrate. Ideally the physical

---

41 Restoring any negative thoughts and actions taken into positive ones i.e. serving others selflessly.

body is cremated, which makes way for a clean, clear departure of the spirit from the physical domain.

When the physical body is artificially kept alive, as is often the case when a person is in a coma the spirit and soul are unable to depart. As long as there is blood flowing (artificially) through the veins there is life, soul contact will remain and neither the spirit nor the soul can return to the source. This for me is a tragedy for the soul as it cannot leave due to its vibration being artificially kept alive.

The spirit's relationship to the physical body

I believe that most people feel that there is a spirit within their physical body. But many may not realise that it is this very force, their spiritual force, which is responsible for all body movement. It is the driving force which lies behind every physical act, this I term "the spiritual will". It is a different force to that of physical willpower. One of the differences between the spiritual and physical willpower is that physical willpower is logically based and takes energy from the physical body, whilst spiritual power is spiritually based and is directed by the soul. This gives energy to the physical body. These different types of willpower also determine the vitality of the etheric body (the electromagnetic field of energy, i.e. life force) that helps to enhance and motivate the physical body towards its divine purpose.

For as long as the soul decides to be present within the physical body then the spirit must also remain intact, the etheric flow - electromagnetic – is still kept active by the soul. The spirit within is only able to leave the physical body when full physical death occurs, whereby the physical body begins to degenerate. When physical death has occurred the spirit will hover (float) around the physical body for up to seven days. However this is a figure that may vary, in relation to what may remain to be done from a soul level.

During the period of mourning, the cultural energy of placing flowers on the body of the deceased, on the coffin or alongside the side the grave has a deeper meaning from a spiritual perspective. The energy of the flowers actually helps to release the spirit from any attachment it may have towards the physical body. The vibration of the flowers greatly aids the spirit's release, taking it outwards and upwards towards its own transition. The Egyptians had an insight into the meaning of this, which was why they took such great steps to preserve the physical body by embalming it. By embalming the physical body they virtually stopped its natural process of disintegration, preventing its return to the earth. Because of this the spirit of the deceased was - in many cases - unable to fully leave the presence of what had been its living temple due to its attachment to it. That is why curses that were placed on the burial chambers by the priests and the then-living ruler remained strong. Such curses would come into power when those burial chambers were broken into or looted. With that kind of attachment regarding body and spirit, it is no wonder that such places have a strong presence of being haunted. Over the years the embalming would begin to disintegrate and the natural degeneration of the body would begin, thus releasing the spirit also.

I can recall one occasion, when I was resting near my mother's open coffin during the wake and my mother's spirit was flying around me in the room. I connected with her telepathically and asked her to let go of any attachments she may have had to her home and family, to which she agreed. Upon the last night of her rest before transition was completed, I heard her footsteps as she went around the house opening and closing some of the doors. For me, it was a beautiful experience to realise that her period of readjustment was complete. I was laughing to myself as it was happening whilst I lay downstairs in my temporary bed next to her coffin.

The spirit of any person (depending upon its transitional period) will after a number of days, eventually rise from the consciousness of the earth plane in order to return to the melting pot of universal consciousness. The spirit of the individual dissolves and fades into the universal consciousness to become at one with all again. For me, this demonstrates that the body of the spirit is not a permanent energy force, indicating again that it is a tool and a servant of the soul.

The soul's connection to the physical body

The soul's urge to serve: If the general urge in the life of humanity is to satisfy basic desires and needs, the urge to serve is an equally basic principle of the soul of all human beings. But this latter part is seldom satisfied. To serve and obey the soul is a way forward in spiritual development, to seek and step out of the shadows of the lower nature into enlightenment. The soul has not returned to earth in order to fulfil the wishes of the lower nature: that is the ego's desires. The ego's desires can be accomplished quickly, but what then? What is there left to do? Boredom quickly follows, for boredom is the killer of the passion of life.

There are certain dark areas that the initiate should be aware of as they seek to implement their spiritual soul practice:

1: The elimination of prejudices, national and religious pride.

2: The recognition of shortcomings, such as anger.

3: To have a spirit of tolerance and forgiveness.

4: Refuse to be afraid of any results of right and positive action.

5: Fear lies behind all that you mistrust. It gives birth to false attitudes. Fear kills truth.

6: Do not be afraid of those who seek to kill the body, but look for those who seek to dominate the soul.

7: Now that you have sensed the vision and recognised the hindrances which try to block your way, you are then ready to deal with the inner fears. This will become a part of what must be created in you in order to become free from it.

8: It is important to identify yourself constructively with human pain. If, for example you were to react violently to any situation, darkness still lies within. In such situations you would have lost the deeper connection of soul meaning. The way of many is always to react through the emotions, which can create a stronger negative force between those involved. By trying to disarm any situation through higher insight, peaceful means and compassion, the true way for change can be created.

9: When sympathy is used in such a way that does not produce positive action of some kind, it can become a festering sore in the side of the individual. It is only by right thought, deed, and word that the lover of humanity will enter the battle against the negative forces that help mirror that truth. Seek with all your heart to understand the light of eternal life with peace and joy.

The soul's transition from the physical body is usually quite straightforward when death is manifested by the force of the soul (see *Ways of dying* on next page). But it can be different when the body has been destroyed in a particularly violent way, such as being blown up by a bomb. This can have a strong negative effect upon the spirit and soul bodies of the person due to the violence of the force. It would also be difficult for the soul to fully collect itself whilst the violent vibration was still active, but when that vibration recedes, restoration is completed. It is also true to say that there is no such thing as an accident. I personally see it as a "happening". And if there is a happening whereby the individual is experiencing a death situation outside of a natural death, it will adjust to the situation.

Whenever the physical body is artificially kept alive by medical intervention (as is often the case with coma patients) it actually prevents the soul from fully leaving the physical body. Under such circumstances the soul will stay in close proximity (hovering over) of the physical body, waiting for the moment when it can leave in its natural form. The soul will seek ways (depending on the circumstances) to detach itself from the physical body in order to create physical death. The soul has the ability to close down a vital organ or organs, such as the kidneys, or it can stop the flow of blood via the heart in order to fully detach itself from the physical plane, thus causing death. It may even try to break the central nervous system through snapping the nadis that flows from the spleen, which is why sometimes a coma patient is seen to shake violently for a period of time.

Ways of dying

The soul leaves the body at the moment of physical death in three ways, for the following reasons:

1: Through the solar plexus – for a life that is usually based on emotional content.

2: Through the heart centre – for a life that is usually connected to a loving caring nature.

3: Through the head area or consciousness – for a life of greater mental activity that may contain both of the above.

In the above three categories it also indicates what kind of life an individual may have lived prior to death, as is given very briefly with each example of departure. It can also be indicative of what illness (if any) may be related to the cause of death, such as bowel cancer, heart attack or a brain tumour. The heart attack, for example, can be a clean painless way of departing, which is also a positive indication that the person will have lived a life of goodness and service. A specific disease may also occur by the soul as a means of departing the earth. This aspect of viewing death can only be understood and accepted if you are not connected to seeing suffering or pain from a purely physical point of view. I see physical death as a transition from one plane of consciousness into another: yes, physical death is a rebirth.

When physical death has occurred in a natural manner,[42] then there is a natural way forward for the soul and spirit to depart the physical body as complete energy forms. The soul and spirit are then able to journey upwards and away from the earth plane, firstly passing through the darkness of the underworld (a ring of negative energy that surrounds the earth). The soul then returns to its original place of creation in the universal consciousness - be it to another world, another galaxy or another universe. In this manner the soul differs from

42 During sleep or a heart attack.

the energy of the spirit, the spirit is a temporary energy and is reabsorbed back into the collective consciousness of the universe.

There are a number of bands of energy that surround the earth world, each connected to universal consciousness. As mentioned, the first band of energy that is outside the earth's aura, closest to the earth is a dark band known as the *underworld*. It is not, as is often suggested, beneath the earth in the ground; it is the universal underworld.

The underworld is a band of energy made up of the dark forces of lower-natured spirits. Many of the "masters of the original evil" dwell in this energy field. A dwelling place could be a house or tavern where a negative force or forces find their own particular place of consciousness. It is as if they are in their own prisms, as I have experienced whilst working in this vibration. Such places may attract similar forms of consciousness whilst maintaining their appearance as a physical being, in an ethereal form. Soul beings or spirits who find themselves in the underworld will have created strong negative energies - such as murder - whilst walking the earth, and as such will have amassed much negative karma. Such spirits do not wish to journey up into the light in order to look at what they have created in that lifetime or previous ones. They also do not want to face their own karma in order to reach for higher planes of consciousness to transform it. They chose to remain with like minded souls in their own domain, thus avoiding taking responsibility for what they created, in that or indeed other lifetimes. This can be an ongoing as long as they choose to remain in a negative dark vibration. In many respects this darkness is mirrored on earth by those who are caught up in, or purposefully manifest, evil and darkness for their own gain.

Those that remain in the shadow of the underworld seek opportunities to return to earth other than by karmic pull. They may choose to return by the route of possession and haunting, and poltergeists are such energies. Dark forces (such as negative thoughts and dark individuals) are unable to penetrate the universal consciousness of truth, love and compassion, unless the consciousness holds a negative vibration. All negative, dark and evil energies bounce back off the outer circle of light, back into the dark ring and back towards earth. So there is no escape other than to return to the light. This is partly why the earth is holding so much negative karma. The transformational work - evil to goodness - must be carried out on earth through divine connections. The consciousness of the earth is in quarantine until all evil has been transformed. This is a universal law which protects other dimensions from becoming corrupted by evil.

Those that choose the opposite and follow their natural path of spiritual growth when death occurs will break or pass through that darkness into the light of guidance. However it is important to understand that a negative spirit may choose to appear before an individual or a healer for such a transmission. In this light the negative force may not seek you out to create fear or to possess you, but instead has appeared to find a way through the band of negative forces with the help of your love and light. Anyone with a clear consciousness (lack of fear, or darkness within themselves) can send any dark energy into the ray of light. If a person has darkness within themselves they are often unable to do such work but can be guided, as universal law states. This subject matter is much deeper than is being expressed here and I will address it further on.

There is a natural transition that the soul follows to return to a place of rest in the universe. That place of restitution could be in another world, planet or galaxy or to whichever dimension the soul belongs. Upon arrival, the soul will firstly reclaim its awareness of being fully conscious on another vibratory level (without the attachment of the physical aspect), and secondly, reassess its position regarding the manner in which it may continue its journey. When the readjustment period is complete, the soul will receive guidance and help from a higher being; no one is left unattended. The period of rest may be for a number of earth weeks, days or years. This is determined firstly by the consciousness of the soul in relation to the master's guidance. When acceptance has been achieved regarding the next step to be taken, a route of return is once again taken by the soul, and rebirth occurs on earth.

No soul is ever forced to perform or do anything that it does not wish to do; this also includes those souls that remain in the dark band of energy around the world. Many find this concept difficult to understand and often ask "Why don't the light worker just go in and clear all of the evil?" But few realise that there is a deep karmic meaning behind darkness, the hidden, light and truth. True spirit does not interfere; it will help only when asked to do so. An opportunity to return to the light is always present for the lost souls of the underworld, but more often than not it is rejected. My help has often been rejected by the dark forces, and I have had to leave them to their own recourses, trusting that a way forward into the light will eventually be seen by those who are trapped and eluded by their own illusions.

Chapter 7

The Ego and the Three Planes of Consciousness

Ego is the poison of the soul: There are two forms of ego that are created from the same source. They are the ego of the lower nature, the 3D consciousness and its personality, and the spiritual ego that is connected to the 3D and 4D consciousnesses. You must first establish an egoless higher personality by living it before you can access and establish fifth dimensional consciousness (5D). The 5D-being is an individual who is able to hold their vibration to be fully present at all times, who is then totally free from the lower nature; it is a constant state of harmony with all things, that of enlightenment.

Ego's connection to the lower mind: the lower mind is a denser form of consciousness, meaning that the consciousness is vibrating on the lower frequency of light (physical) to that of higher consciousness. It is aligned to the five physical senses and earth laws of time, distance and matter. The lower mind's orientations are purely physical, logical box thinking, and it views life this way.

The lower mind's thought patterns resonate on the practical issues of life that are mechanical. The survival factor is its strongest instinct that has an understanding of mortality not immortality. It is deeply connected to your feelings towards the natural world, types of food eaten and drunk, politics, religion and relationships which form its identity, that of lower personality.

Density is governed by gravity, which coerces (compels) light or photons into form. The lower mind holds the densest level of consciousness and is therefore fixed to its location within the boundaries of physiological forms and to the meaning of life through physicality.

The ego's home is in the lower mind and emotions. It can only play by the rules of the 3D consciousness. Within this field of energy, which includes the five physical senses and physical laws, there are to be found the timescales of past, present and future. Between them they cohere with the choices that are made on this level of thought. Each individual holds an identity which I refer to as "lower personality". How much you identify yourself with your lower personality determines how strong an ego you will hold. For a variety of reasons it must be said that the emotional body is strongly connected to the ego. Needs, fears, desires, expectations, and taking things personally, staying in the dramas and seeing oneself as a victim are but a few ways in which the ego seeks to control the lower personality through the emotions. These all vibrate on the 3D consciousness which seeks to hold on to its identity and keep you in the dark. Fear activates many of the emotional responses that are so present in today's societies.

Your feelings are also connected to the past through certain experiences (not necessarily of this life), but your feelings resonate on a higher vibration to your emotions. Feelings are transformed emotions that no longer cloud your view of life. Your feelings are connected to your intuition and heart. By listening to your feelings you are working through a higher vibration of consciousness.

Thought, logic, emotions and ego reside within the periphery of 3D consciousness. This is a tricky combination to overcome because it is strongly motivated by the elements described here. But let us look more closely to the ego and the logical mind. Logic is fixed to the laws of past, present and future. The identity (lower personality) will to a great degree of the time (eighty per cent or more) coexist between the past and future. If you are more aware of your habits (thought patterns) you may spend some fifteen per cent of your daily time being present. Within the remaining eighty-five per cent there is a great mixture of emotions and fears that are continually going around and around in your mind and emotions seeking solutions to daily living. This is where the ego seeks to dominate the life patterns by continually relating itself to past events through judgement with the wish to control the future, or at the very least, make it right. However there is one place where the ego does not wish to be – in the present! Why? If the ego were to step into the present it would have nothing to do, it would be virtually redundant, out of a job. For this not to happen, the ego will fight every aspect of light (consciousness) that seeks to liberate it from itself.

One of the strongest tools that the ego uses to keep itself in power (identity) is judgement. Judgement justifies everything to the ego, the likes of which are: I like this, I don't like that. This is good, that is bad. You are wrong I am right! Judgement is based on 3D, that of black or white, right or wrong, much of which can be experienced in today's society. It is not a cosmic right to judge anything or anyone, for nothing is black or white; there is always the unseen and the unknown. I realise that I am touching on a very sensitive point here, but if you ask yourself, "Who is complete enough to judge another person?" you can find your answer in the Bible where it states "Let he without sin cast the first stone." The transformation of the consciousness of judgement into acceptance is an important key, one that can be used to release the ego from itself.

You cannot truly love if you have an ego identity. The ego is like a cloaked shadow that covers the soul's ability to love. Ask yourself how many identities you are holding on to. An identity could be a belief system, anger towards another person or a particular type of person. It could be as simple as not liking what a person wears or even their hair style! If, or when you say to yourself or another (friend), "Look at what she or he is wearing, how can they wear that?" you are most definitely in your ego. This is a darkness that is being carried by you because any form of judgement creates separation. It matters not if the other person does not hear you (on a physical level); it is still registered by that person on a psychic level because the energy, your thoughts, will have touched their psyche. You have separated yourself from that person, not only on a physical level but also spiritually. This is a common phenomenon with those who are not living their lives beyond the 3D. Judgement is a form of darkness that can be transformed simply by accepting!

The ego likes being noticed, and being seen to be achieving.

It is true that through achieving certain experiences are gained, and experience is the best teacher of life. But if achieving is based purely on competitiveness (much of the school philosophy taught today is based on this principle), then trouble may lie ahead. For example, from an early age children are taught to compete against each other, for example by achieving good exam results to become top of the class. If you want to become the greatest guitar player in the world, there is no reason why you may not achieve that. With enough practice it may be possible. But what happens after that? The next day or a week later there may be someone else who can play even better than you. What then?

In all aspects of life it is important to ask yourself some basic questions, such as what is this teaching me? Does it bring me joy? What am I learning by following this line of thought? Am I helping others or am I simply taking from others? Everything that you do or think of is a creative force. We touch each other in this way; we are connected. Energy is everywhere, but how is it enhanced? You know from deep within that the materialistic aspects of life, such as owning a car, house, boat and a wardrobe full of clothes are but temporary fulfilments. The looks of a car do not fulfil the deepest part of you; it is only a lump of metal that has been modelled in such a way to make you believe that it is perfect for you (in accordance with fashion). But a week or a month or two later you may not see it in the same way; it may have become familiar to your needs and will eventually become just another car! What then? Do you buy the latest model to fulfil the ego's need to be satisfied for another short period of time? This, for me, is what consumerism and materialism has created - a bottomless pit of needs and desires! Individuals can often become attached to material things, which act as a surrogate for self love. The focus can be turned away from personal sharing with others into personal needs that become an increasing important aspect of the ego's identity!

Cultural programming of the ego: an example of this is how in Western cultures, enormous pressure (through advertising and fashion) has been laid on adolescent and young people alike to look a certain way. This includes buying a great variety of products from clothes to make up that carry a specific "label". This is the ego's vanity trap! Why? Because it is all based on outer recognition. But what is happening with the inner-self? You may have the most beautiful-looking and beautifully-dressed person in front of you, but that person may have little depth of personality. The ego will soon become bored with the outer reflection, and what then, do you look for someone that may seem even more beautiful? If you become a shell of outer appearances, where is the soul? Beauty on the outside is like a passing cloud; it eventually fades away and becomes something else. In this area (outer appearance) the ego can become so strong that eternal youth is much sought after. Beyond the flood of face and skin creams that profess eternal youth, to the extremes of plastic surgery, where does the insecurity come from? I would say a distinct lack of spiritual maturity. Have you noticed that it is becoming increasingly difficult to find a person that is gracefully growing older, someone that holds the air of natural looking skin and hair colour that complements their age!

There is a whole industry that feeds the ego through identity. There is a natural look that everyone has. A look that is far deeper; you shine from within. I am not saying that a person should not wear lipstick or powder their faces or even dye their hair. Like with all things of this nature, it is extremism that demonstrates the truth.

The ego is greedy in all respects: the ego has an unquenchable appetite for attention and recognition. Due to this, the ego is a creator of separation and negativity. There is always a price to pay for the ego's persona, emotionally and mentally. The ego can be heard – saying, "No, you are not getting away with it," or it can be softer

– such as suggesting that you please someone in order to be accepted. These are the dualities that arise from past experiences that each individual has to contend with on a daily basis. The grip of the ego will remain with the individual for as long as 3D consciousness is based on the likes of needs, fear and expectations. When the ego has a grip over the psyche in this manner, the attempt to escape or transform it may be temporary. Escapism could involve burying your feelings or burying your head in the sand like the ostrich. Escapism can also lead to you becoming cold and hard to others, which may be due to you having been deeply hurt at some time in your life. Escapism is a method of protection; by itself it does not change a thing, it is a delay tactic.

As mentioned before, the physical will is logically orientated. An example of this is when you may be driven to get something done at all costs, which can be at the cost of your own time of taking care of the self. It can also have a negative effect on others if you push them aside to get it done. You can often find the perfectionist at work here. One of the ways that the ego escapes giving another person responsibility is for the perfectionist to say "I will do it to save time because I know what I am doing". With the perfectionist there is no room for error! But perhaps more importantly, by not allowing others to make mistakes, the ego does not trust itself on a deeper level.

Control is a major factor of the ego's behaviour and eventually leads to symptoms of stress. We live in an increasingly stressful society, mainly because of the ego's continual need to achieve. The physical downside is endemic in our societies at large, which is mirrored by our not accepting our differences. The upside is that it has now reached the point where humanity is being forced to look at life in other ways or else self-destruct. It is no longer enough to look at life on the outside (the reflection), you need to also examine what is going on within you now. You have to explore your emotions and fears in order to transform them. The ego's transformation can begin by the individual working on the inner self to raise their consciousness. The ego does the opposite by judging, this is the classic way of escaping responsibility for how you think, act and react to others! Examples of the ego's narrow ways of thinking are shown if you say to another person, "I don't like you in those clothes, why don't you change them?" Or "It's your fault, you did this, and so you fix it." Instead of judgement, how about working together, then there may be an opportunity for real change to take place.

In the corporate world there is much talk about teamwork. However, true teamwork is only possible if there is no ego present on any level. If there is, then competitiveness may be present between individuals, shown, for example, in power struggles for position.

Being ego-less is essentially about clearing all shadows from your life, a shadow being anything that is negative or judgemental. The higher self holds the personality of your 4D consciousness that already knows the way to liberate you from your ego; it has the tools to help you do this. It holds the power of truth because it is the truth. Whenever you are true to the self, it must follow that it is true for others around you; you speak from your heart.

The ego cannot remain in the light because light strips it of its identity and the shadow falls away. All shadows (negativity) are illusions created by 3D consciousness. The shadow-self seeks to hold and control you through lower irrational consciousness. An example of this is how the ego (shadow) will try to block or reject your greater sense of trusting the self, your inner faith. Faith in this context is not a religious concept, but an inner knowing, a deeper sense of trust, a knowing of what is true that vibrates beyond fear! Learning to hold the vibration of trust is not an easy task. It requires a greater sense of discipline that seeks to take the 3D across the bridge of life into your 4D orientation. It is impossible to obtain true liberty of the lower self through your 3D. Your 3D orientation does not have the necessary tools to accomplish such a transformation of consciousness rising. As mentioned earlier, the ego does not want to be fully present where the identity of itself becomes meaningless!

To transform the ego essentially means to raise your consciousness from the 3D conditioning you have been taught to obey. You may be just waking up to seeing life through spiritual orientation[43] rather than the ego's. Or you may have been following the spiritual path for a number of years. It matters not, what is important is that the inner journey of self-realisation, your awakening, has begun! You will find the necessary tools to help you on this path of self development towards the liberation you seek through spiritual means. I would even say that you already have the necessary tools but may not have realised it. Have you opened the doors of your temple (such as heart and mind) to enlighten them with wisdom? When you enter a dark room you put on the light and the darkness disappears, this is a universal law at work. When you enter a room that is connected to your emotional body and put on the light, you may find a shadow in the corner, something you were not aware of before. Let us call it anger. The anger may have been there for a long time, but you chose not to look at it in

---

43 Questioning your motives, the way you do things, being present in all that you do. Learn to relax by accepting what comes your way in life.

a responsible way. For whatever reason, you may have used anger as a tool to manipulate or change things in your environment, such as your workplace or at home. Then one day a thought of higher conscious came and lit up that room. You then began to question your motives in life because you realised that there was a shadow hidden in the corner of the emotional self and you were willing to work on it.

To understand the motives behind your feelings is a step closer to the liberation you seek. The ego and all dark forces require their influences to be fed: fear, judgement, criticism and doubt are but a few. A dark force continually searches for and creates negativity. The negativity drains you of your energy. You stay tired because you remain negative in your thoughts and outlook on life. This can occur when you choose to stay in the drama or continue to see yourself as the victim of life; both are elements of the past. It may seem impossible to let go of those emotions and thoughts. You may find yourself asking, *why can't I let go of these thoughts and emotions?* But there is a way to transform the negative if you are willing to communicate with your shadow. If you are willing to communicate with your lower nature then you have to open the door for the real change to take place. Any shadow, any doubt that you are holding will not move by itself; it requires right thinking. You, your light (soul consciousness), have to lift any doubts or fears up into your higher consciousness (symbolic of crossing the bridge into 4D) to be able to transform the way you think and feel about yourself. In this manner you are taking the necessary steps to rewire your brain by creating new neural connections from the left to the right hemisphere of your brain. This automatically draws more light into your consciousness and new neuron connections are established. For example, when fear arises within and you recognise it as your shadow standing in front of you, you can communicate with it. You can tell the shadow to stand behind you because you are moving forward and passing through the fear, because it can no longer influence you taking a positive step.

Taking responsibility for your choices is another important step towards transforming the ego. For example, projection and rejection are close allies! Whatever you choose to do in any given situation, in any given moment, has a definite effect upon everything that you receive in life. In other words your thoughts go before you. Yes, action and reaction, cause and effect follow the choices you make! When the calling card returns to you, i.e. what you send out comes back; you may have forgotten what you asked for some time ago. And what comes back often differs from your expectations. This is because the universe is not interested in fulfilling your needs or emotional demands; it only supports what is true i.e. selflessness. The mirrors of life are abundant, but the ego does not wish to look at its own reflection and will prevent itself from doing so, by, for example, blaming another person for what has happened. You get back what you send out, what you do to others you do to yourself - these are basic universal laws, which to a great degree are not understood or at worst ignored in human affairs. If they were fully understood and acted upon it would not be possible to judge another! These laws and principles should be taught in all schools, globally, as a means to help eliminate the ego so that all beings can live as brother and sister in harmony with each other and nature.

The universe is far wiser that we give it credit for. Universal laws are not logically accepted simply because they go beyond the threshold of rational ability to choose rather than decide. An example of the human's arrogance is depicted in global warming. The ego believes that it can make a contract with nature by choosing to ignore the science behind the facts that the world is heading for a global disaster. This is exacerbated by the lack of will to make real change happen, such as by collecting all discarded plastics. The oceans of the world are fast becoming a plastic soup as plastic particles are broken down by sunlight. Another fact is that globally, there is eighty-nine per cent more money spent on arms,[44] which is based on fear - to protect at all costs - rather than on green technology that would make the world self-sufficient in power.

The conditioned logical mind has become so far removed from its connection to the Gaia (earth's energy), and the intuitive qualities of the higher mind, that it has become mentally extreme (overactive) in its mechanistic thinking. This is witnessed by the way that the various sciences of the day express their points of view, where esoteric science is often frowned upon, and where the more open holistic approach to science and life itself is shunned. This is an area where the ego has a strong foothold, whereby ignorance or the lack of acceptance of alternative means is at times extreme. Ego corrupts through material and monetary gains. But there is a way out of such extremism, which applies to all humanity. When you, as an individual become self-realised you are connected to the whole – universal consciousness – and as such will not take anything personally. Neither will you pursue material gain at the cost of another. This alone will help liberate you from any ego that may be controlling the lower self. You will realise that what comes to you is a gift and as such is not an attack upon

44 In global politics there are double standards. Some countries provide aid for war-torn countries whilst at the same time providing arms to the perpetrators. This is evil as all arms are connected to the dark side.

your personal self because there is a message behind it. Every experience you have offers an opportunity for greater change to take place.

Through your consciousness raising you realise increasingly that what comes to you, comes as a message. You are then able to look behind what is presented to you, which will help take you beyond logic and into intuitional variants.

If, for example, someone is angry with you - for whatever reason - that person is not angry with you, but with themselves. Somewhere within that person there is a battle taking place because their ego was hurt. You could try asking the person why they are angry with you (giving back their power and responsibility). They may offer excuses to project the fault upon you. You may then return with the answer, "No it's not that again", and in this way you give them back their responsibility for being angry with you, creating an opportunity for change! Then a real dialogue may come from your stance of not accepting another person's anger by not taking it personally - you have gone beyond the ego's control. Ego and anger require feeding; they feed off the energies of other people. All dark forces do this! If you became angry back with the person who was angry with you, you will have fallen into that trap; you are feeding it by reacting in a negative manner. This is where revenge emanates from the old consciousness of, "An eye for an eye; or tooth for a tooth" which is no longer relevant to the increasing numbers of spiritually-orientated, higher minded people.

Revenge is a destructive energy that has not yet reached its peak in human evolution, which is why so many wars are taking place globally! When you, as an individual, begin to develop and learn to hold and maintain your 4D consciousness you automatically become more present. The more present you become, the more you will realise that there is no such thing as negativity. The illusion will have been recognised by you and you will stop playing games with yourself and others. Now that is a big step into the light, welcome home!

The spiritual ego: the spiritual ego seeks to control and block your true channelling by stopping you from being present. In this manner it clouds your inner ability to access the consciousness of the higher self. The true higher-self is your higher personality where the ego is not present. The lower nature, continually seeks recognition and identity to confirm its presence. This is not true for someone who is self-less. For example, the healer who is self-less is a server of truth, one without identity but present in the light. Identity requires conformation. For example, the guru is a creation of the ego, which often becomes the ego of the masses. The guru can be self-professed, as in, **Look at me or look at who I am.** The followers who idolise the guru literally place that person on the platform, along with the big chair or sofa. Then the ego feels that it is in the right orientation! Here is a fact - **When a guru becomes a guru, the guru is no longer a guru.** There is no such thing as a guru; the guru is an illusion of the ego.

It is only right that on your spiritual path you should seek wisdom from those who you feel can share and empower you with their spiritual wisdom, in order to help your spiritual development. But it becomes another thing when the personality gets in its way (your or their ego). Being truly humble emanates from the heart that caries clear expression of higher mind principles. Spirituality for me is not about how great you think you are it is about how to emanate love and knowledge to empower those seeking enlightenment through your guidance. Enlightenment can only occur through your own experiences and inner transformation of your chakra centres.

Any spiritual teacher or guru who tells you that they can enlighten you in one day, week, month or year is not being true to themselves or you. Are you aware of the depth of what enlightenment means?

Hypothetically, if I were to say to you, "Come to my course and I will enlighten you this weekend," would you come? Whether you came or not would of course depend largely upon your needs and what attracts you to me. This in itself is a loaded situation! But let us get back to the basic question of my claim to enlighten you. From my experience, insights and understanding of how the various fields of energies orientate themselves, I would not be able to directly enlighten you over any given amount of time. To do this would mean that I would have to take into myself and hold the energies of every thought you have ever had and all experiences you have ever lived through. I would be responsible for all of them. Can you begin to imagine how much karma I would have to hold to free you from your own responsibility? Even if that were possible, what would be left within you? You would be empty of your own experiences. How would you be able to respond to and understand life's situations without your experiences? Of course this is not possible; there would be a great void, a distinct lack of *Self.* This is where many people who seek enlightenment through another often lose sight of themselves. The individual seeking enlightenment through another is in fact giving their power away to that person or ideal. *I know of no living person who is developed enough to directly enlighten another.*

From an energy perspective, what I understand to be happening in this situation is that when an individual attends an enlightenment course for a short period of time (a weekend, week or a month) some energy, such as emotions and feelings, may have moved or are moved by following certain practices. Meditation and the use of the breath are often used to raise energy levels. The individual may feel a strong shift of energy, as for example in the sense of feeling lighter or uplifted. This may last for the whole period of their stay at the ashram, centre or workshop. But what happens when that person leaves the energies of an ashram or spiritual centre and re-enters the life of normal everyday 3D living? For example, if the individual has not done their inner-work, then certain chakras will not have received the correct vibrations needed to transform them, and the emotional body may not have been transformed from any negative influences. The individual may not have gone through a total transformation of the energies and vibrations of those areas. Sooner or later (a week, weeks, or even a month) the old energy will again rise to express itself (as it must) in order to seek recognition and release.

In other words, the inner and transformational work of the chakras (light consciousness) must come from within yourself; no other person can do that for you. If a spiritual teacher or guru claims that they can enlighten you, I would advise you to walk the other way, and in doing so save your time and money!

Directly or indirectly there is a certain amount of ego involved in those who claim to be able to do such things, which is also true for those who seek a quick way to enlightenment. *A quick path to enlightenment is not possible. You may get a quick fix (uplifting of your energies) but you will have to keep on returning to have another fix*. This can become addictive and as such you will continually give your power away instead of looking within through self-awareness. One of the positive things that happen when you are continually looking outside the self for enlightenment is that you will get some kind of confirmation of where you need to go. You may even get a "wow" moment or two and celebrate. But do not become attached to it, whatever it may be. Otherwise the ego will become present again. Trust your feelings!

A word of warning: false (dark) spiritual helpers and guides can corrupt the channel of the one who holds the vibration of the ego whilst working spiritually or through normal consciousness. An example of this is when an individual may have strong psychic powers, but is not as yet clear from their emotional responses and ego. The psychic energies give access to higher vibration forces, such as intuition and possibly the clairvoyant and clairaudient faculties. But the lower nature of the person may not yet have been mastered. Because the ego seeks recognition and conformation, the psychic person may be able to read the other person's energies (such as the aura), but will not necessarily be able to restrain or use the insight in a respectful manner. I have had such people coming up to me and begin by telling me my life story, or giving an energy reading without me asking for it or perhaps more importantly, asking me if it is OK to give me a reading! Now that is a big ego! Under such circumstances the ego has moved its location from logic to the intuitive. But the need of the ego is still based in the lower mind and emotions with a spiritual basis, which obviously has not been transformed into higher consciousness. This kind of reading is not true channelling, it is a psychic reading, which is of a much lower vibration. Nothing is new, the person giving the reading is simply confirming things you already know, but presenting them to you in a different way. And you believe they are channelling when they are not reaching out into your higher domains to give true guidance and wisdom sharing.

Dark spiritual helpers and guides are not true to the light; they are false but will disguise themselves to make the one channelling believe that they are true light beings. This can be because the ego of the one channelling wants it to be true or they are not advanced enough for such work. I have been in the presence of many people who have fallen onto this trap of working with false guides. They can read the energies of any individual and therefore know if there is a weakness. They will play on those weaknesses to gain more power over the individual. Let's say for example that you have a friend who keeps on phoning you (any time of the day or night) to tell you what their guide has just said. You may eventually ask yourself why that person keeps calling you. The answer is pretty clear to me; ego requires conformation of its power at all times! Then an individual channelling may be led into the darkness by seeking recognition. As you may be aware, there is a circle of energy here as it keeps coming back to the ego's powers of persuasion to dominate the true feelings.

Here are some of the negative aspects of spirituality that come from the same source. These are sources of the original evil that tries to keep you away from true service by seeking to keep you in the dark. Ego is based upon personal identity. The ego continually tries to control what you feel through your physical as well as higher senses, until it has been transformed and mastered by the higher self.

Some of the tools that the ego uses to control you are:

1: *Jealousy* – one of the most destructive forces that anyone can hold.

2: *Judgement* – of the lower mind, logical. One sees the world as black or white, right or wrong? It is a very destructive energy. No one person can judge another. Judgement is not a universal law; it is the ego's way of creating separation.

3: *Fear* – seeks to take you away from the light and your inner faith by creating doubt.

4: *Envy* – you want what someone else has but may not be willing to work for? Envy and jealously are closely linked.

5: *Greed* – deep emotional dissatisfaction, cannot have enough.

6: *Comparing* – the mirror of oneself to others, wanting to be like another person or not.

7: *Insecurity* – a deep lack of trust, instability mentally, emotionally and spiritually.

The ego's purpose is to separate you from your soul guidance and the harmony it brings to your mind and heart.

Ways in which to transform the ego

An important step in transforming the ego is to first admit or recognise that you have one. From there you can begin your inner-self study. One such study is becoming more responsible for the choices and actions you take on a daily basis. This will give you insight into behaviour patterns that are ego based. From there you can look at how to make the necessary changes that will free you from the control patterns you may find yourself caught up in, such as fear. It is wise to remember that the dark side will in all ways try to keep you out of the light of higher consciousness because it is seeking to guide you through your heart, the place of compassion. The ego has many ways in which it tries to control your life force - fear and doubt being two. Whenever you are in doubt, confusion is present. When you are confused, you are not in your power or light - *the shadow has fallen.* Fear can arise from confusion, which may take you further away from your inner truth. It can even lead you into the selfishness of the "I"- only me, which is a part of the ego's identity.

What is the energy of doubt? Doubt could be referred to as hesitation; hesitation is a pause, a moment of mental and emotional confusion. In the confusion you may try to assess (logically) the situation and what to do next, which is not a moment of contemplation; contemplation does not carry the vibration of doubt. It could be a moment where fear arises. Or is it a moment of higher thought orientation that holds no fear? Contemplative moments that are held without fear are peaceful moments, ones of seeking to understand and decide upon an issue rather than rationalise. Doubt creates over-rationalisation that will take you into choices (back into the black or white scenario). The choices are to a great degree controlled by your conditioning, and there can be a whole lifetime of inner work to be done in order to transform the thousands of years of your conditioning over many lifetimes. So be patient and kind to the self; few have managed to make such a major transformation in a single lifetime - although it is said the Lord Jesus Christ experienced twenty seven lifetimes in one! Now that is some karma to transform.

The confused mind is a clouded mind that contains elements of fear. I would suggest that it is often the emotions, which arise at times of doubt, that add to the confused state of mind. The emotions confuse your thoughts and are not the thoughts themselves. Yes, if allowed to, emotion can flood the mental body of the lower consciousness, creating chaos! An extreme example of this is when an individual becomes an emotional thinker resulting in jealousy. The emotional thinker has a lack of clarity from the mental plane. Most choices are based on the needs and fears of the individual i.e. past experiences and future speculations.

One physical symptom of this is an imbalanced thyroid gland. An individual with thyroid imbalance often finds it difficult to make clear choices; they lack the physical willpower to manifest their wishes and are in a general state of confusion about their life's purpose. They often find it difficult to get motivated in general, lack self confidence, and continually search outside themselves for answers, solutions or conformation. Because the thyroid gland is ruled by the throat chakra, the individual with a thyroid imbalance often lacks the power of expression through the spoken word. To voice their opinion is difficult (other than in anger) because they doubt themselves. In order to transform doubt it is important to first transform fear. Doubt, like the imbalanced thyroid gland, is a later energy to the original, that of fear. Fear is the shadow that prevents clarity. This is also true of the ego, all fears must be transformed.

Steps of enlightenment:

1: Focus with all your power (light) to TRANSFORM the lower nature to hold a positive vibration i.e. thought. This will help raise your consciousness to a higher vibration of light (from 3D to 4D orientation).

131

2: Activate and balance all chakra centres through methods of meditation and correct use of the breath. This will help to clear all channels where you hold doubts and fears; these are blocking your path to the higher vibration of your soul.

3: Trust in the self and your ability to love the self and others selflessly. You are a true channel of light and have nothing to prove to others. If you do then the ego has become you!

These are a few important steps that you may wish to take in order to be free from the ego's hold over your psyche. You are not truly free to love until the inner work of transforming the ego is accomplished.

Chapter 8

The Underworld

The purpose of this chapter and book is to try to illustrate more clearly what, where and how evil seeks to control and rule world consciousness. Yes, it is that big!

The underworld - as the word may suggest - is not literally to be found under the ground in demonic settings, as is often depicted in the movies or in literature. But some of what is written and illustrated in movies is often very close to what I have personally experienced on many levels. During the years of following my path in life, I have been guided by spiritual experiences which gave me valuable insight into the many forms of darkness that are present. I believe this has been an important part of my soul journey to serve in this manner. One such form of service that has played a major part in my life is the art of exorcism.

The underworld is a dark band of energy that is just inside the earth's aura. It surrounds the earth world, but its vibration cannot penetrate the earth's aura in order to corrupt the universal consciousness therein. It is the place from which evil seeks ways in which to filter its negative forces into all aspects of life on earth. Evil has many guises - some subtle, some very obvious. Evil is a master of *deception* and as such is cunning. It comes not in peace, neither will it raise the white flag to surrender, it does not know what surrender is. In its totality it is selfish, demanding and will take no heed of your higher thoughts when you are not a hundred per cent in your power, the light.

The forces of the underworld seek to control all that they touch; they will use and manipulate the laws of the occult for their own gain. Just as there are degrees of goodness, there are degrees of darkness. The universal law states that when you seek to control another, you are in fact controlling yourself. For example, whenever you do not respect another you are actually not respecting yourself. This is how you become your own limitations for as long as the ego is present within you. Self love and respect for others are values that the dark brotherhood shuns. But how can anyone begin to transform their ego? An important step is to admit that you may have an ego, or at least recognise that it is there. Many are proud of their identity and what they have gained materially in life. Is this the ego? Pride gives insight to a person's power of achieving. It is one thing to have recognised what you may have achieved or how you look, as in appearance, but it becomes an altered energy when the ego is attached to it because the intent and motive behind it will have changed.

Pride and prejudice are not so far apart when the ego is involved. The ego's vibration is the opposite to that of the soul; it takes not gives. The ego seeks to control others (the soul supports and guides). One way that the ego does this is by judging all things through its preferences. It says to itself through lower mind and emotions, "I like this, I don't like that. You are a nice person, the other person is not." Who decides what you may prefer? Ego and evil have similar qualities; they resonate in the lower consciousness in order to control mind and emotions. The ego makes its choices through 3D consciousness. Your soul does not choose because it already knows the way. Your soul decided long ago what your pathway in this lifespan was to be. You are on the earth plane for one reason only which is to develop spiritually by sharing your love and light with others. All that is given in light and peace on the earth is here to support those core values. Ask yourself from deep within your heart, how else can it be? Am I to be a spiritual warrior who bears the light of truth, or a demon of the dark that continually hides to create fear in order to control others? When anyone is in their power (their light), they do not fear any form of judgement. Those who judge you are in their ego and are creating separation.

Globally, these are extremely strong times of change as we have now passed the year 2010. The human psyche is experiencing a strong upturn through the transformational consciousness that every single human being is feeling consciously or unconsciously. Many initiating souls are facing some adverse choices, which is not a negative happening. All events are seeking to take individuals and groups towards first trusting their feelings. From there a bridge can be built which will carry those who are following their inner feelings towards a faith of knowing that the power of love and light is holding everything together. From my experience, in the autumn of 1999 a strong planetary transitional period took place that helped to take earth's consciousness into a higher universal octave. Today global consciousness is being extended to a degree that it feels as if everything is about to fall apart. Materialism and many basic human needs seem to be under threat from many quarters; the financial crash of 2008-2009 is an example of how the greed of the few overpowered their ability to share - drastically affecting the greater majority. These are indeed strong times for any soul to be present on earth.

The consciousness of all light workers - beings of higher consciousness - is gathering into a pool of collective consciousness. Consciousness rising is being established on earth in an effort to transform the negative forces that are presently seeking to control earth consciousness. For example, if you still doubt yourself now, ask: why was I, or am I, unable to let go or move on from the old ways of thinking? Universal wisdom is there to be embraced and enhanced because in every living moment there is opportunity for change. What were you not listening to, or more importantly what were you listening to in those times of opportunity? Was it the ego's fear that created your doubt? *The ego only looks for the end result to justify its purpose, whereas the soul enjoys the experience of the journey.* This is one of the fundamental differences between ego and soul consciousness. Were you holding onto the log that was drifting down the river in 1999, or did you trust and let go to swim to the next opportunity and experience?

The energies emanating from the planets and stars in this your local galaxy and universe are there to guide and help you on your spiritual journey. But you have to make the effort to connect to their source of power, such as through planetary meditation which is connected to your chakras and organs. Since 1999 some of the universal rays of energy have been specifically trying to direct humanity's consciousness towards letting go of the old consciousness in order to embrace the new. The year 2006 was very connected to this transformational principle, but many held on to old behavioural patterns and refused to let go. Due to this, many experienced difficult times physically, mentally and emotionally, and are quite likely to be still doing so. In the latter part of 2007, this energy received a breath of fresh air via the new wave of planetary influences and the pressure seemed to abate. However this was short lived. As 2008 arrived there came an opportunity for deep transformation. For many it was make your mind up time. Maybe you asked yourself who was in charge or wondered how you were now going to take responsibility for yourself and the choices you make.

The reason I ask these questions is to try and emphasise as strongly as I can that your progression towards the light may have felt strong for you. There is no tomorrow left to count on because there never has been, this is one of the illusions of logic. The physical clock is slowly grinding to a halt, whilst the global clock is reaching a climax point before a new age is born. From a universal perspective, the years 2012-15 are of particular interest. So who is going to run the show? Are you going to do what you can in accordance to the universal clock? Or are you going to remain stuck in your past experiences and future projections and speculations?

The year of 2008 was emanating the energies for karmic transformation that were being chiefly directed towards family karma. The year 2009 was a year where opportunity came to be clear about all issues of your life, and to seek clarity regarding those issues. It is my understanding that from the year 2008 until 2023 global consciousness has begun to receive a strong band of energy. It is a wave of universal transformational energy, one that is helping all human beings to enhance their collective karmic consciousness. The moment has come to take on your soul's responsibility to care for all humans as brother and sister. Stop and ask yourself for a moment - what are the options? Keeping your head in the sand – pretending as if nothing is happening? Remaining as you are – playing it safe by sitting on the fence? Or do you get off your --- to do something about your life situation, to accept and move forward by taking positive action about yourself and others?

The earth's karma and your karma will not permit you to remain untouched by what is happening in your environment, another country, continent or globally. There is nowhere to go other than within yourself to find the answers you already have! Why? Because as long as you think negatively and make choices in accordance with those thoughts, you will have a negative effect upon your life and others. An example of this is the question of who elects people into places of power, those ones who make the laws that control through fear. It often turns out that you may not like what has been occurring in your part of the world, but you are not powerless. It can be difficult to live with, but what next? What choices do you make next? Regardless where you may live on this planet, everyone touches each other in some way or other, it is a small place and it is getting smaller.

Until 1999 earth consciousness was preparing itself for a new wave of energy, which was what I called "the wave of karmic exchange". This is what has happened since then! As the light on earth becomes stronger so will negative forces. Those negative forces will try to keep you in the dark about the choices or decisions you may make in relation to your life karma. Hesitation and doubt are levels of consciousness that all beings should be more aware of because they create confusion. By taking your thoughts upstairs into your higher consciousness you will then decide (holistic view) what to do instead of choosing (black or white view). This simple consciousness shift may make a world of difference to your life. Your choices are based upon you seeing life as dualistic (the 3D view); however your decisions have a third element, which contain the insight of higher consciousness.

Your decision making through the higher consciousness ray is holistic in its overview of life. It takes all aspects into account because it is free from the influences of the emotions and ego and therefore evil and darkness cannot be present - clarity and light are.

You may have found the years 1987 to 2010 to have been strong times for the transformation of family karma, not only from within your own family group but for friends as well. If you have an issue with a family member, your father or mother for example, I would recommend that now is the time to resolve and heal the differences created between you. This lifespan is so important to transform all negative emotions. Such emotions may rise from deep within your past in order to be healed. No one person is to blame for anything in life; the person in front of you is in fact you, as you are them! The moment you get into blame, pointing the finger, or saying something is at fault then you are back into darkness. The ego is in charge again because it has managed to separate you from your love; you are lost in your lower mind and emotions and you want to control. Whenever you are back in your past and are lost there (continually focused on it), you are not being present. Then you are not living in the magic of the moment. Everyone has to take greater responsibility for the self in this new wave of Aquarian energy. If you do not, you will be swept away by the flood of mistrust and despair. What are you holding on to? Is it IDENTITY, FEAR, JUDGEMENT of the self and others?

You cannot truly love when you have an identity that is connected to the EGO personality. When the lower personality is corrupted by the ego you are still making choices based on the old consciousness of viewing your experiences as being black or white. It stands then that the ego must be present. And when the ego is present it seeks to control and even corrupt what is within its grasp in order to fulfil its needs - this is a level of darkness. From this perspective you may understand how humanity in general has become lost through the control that the ego has. Evil requires identity in order for it to survive, unlike love and light which just IS. The ego seeks power and it gives power to those who follow it diligently in the belief that it will free them from their misery. It is true to say that the dark brotherhood will reward you in certain ways, such as giving you the feeling of having power over another person or a group. Even this feeling is an illusion, and there is a price to pay. The reward feeds the ego by showing the ego how it can control others through the use of such energies as fear and guilt. The ego likes this and often develops a pattern within individuals, as well as groups, to demonstrate the ego's power to control others. Such a way of life continually seeks justification and rewards for all it does. It is an energy that never sleeps; it will bring you neither peace nor joy. It seeks to take you away from your light, love truth and clarity, and then you may be like a ship drifting into the foggy night without a rudder. And as the Jolly Roger is raised, you are ready to do battle again - but against whom or what, the self?

Darkness can be a lonely place when you hear the waves wash against the shore but are unable to see or touch it. You can become lost in the ego's way of going about its daily business. If you live a life that is dominated by the lower nature, you may remain angry and judgemental of others. Then much transformational work is required on the spiritual path. You inner awakening and calling is by no means impossible to see or hear. Little steps at a time are required to transform the emotional state and lower-mind orientation into feeling and intuitional guidance.

It is possible to rewire the consciousness that keeps you in past dramas and future speculation. By beginning to say no to your emotional responses and yes to positive thoughts the work is being done! Your view (through the physical eyes) is controlled by the lower mind and the thoughts of the lower mind are at least ninety per cent emotionally based. Yes, there is much fear held within the emotions that flood the lower mind with its impulses. An important part of the shift from lower to higher consciousness is to think positively. Nothing is ever personal; what comes to you, you have attracted and it appears for a great purpose. Viewing what comes to you in this manner and being true to yourself is a step that requires constant attention. For example, ask yourself every hour or so, *Where are my thoughts now? In the past or future? Am I being present? Am I thinking 3D or 4D?* When this line of thought-training is followed, you will slowly but surely begin to see results because you are taking responsibility for your emotions and thoughts. To be true to the self is a fundamental law of the universe, without which all else would crumble into the shadows of the underworld.

For me, the orientation of spiritual life is about having the courage to follow my inner calling, to be fearless rather than listening to the ego's demands for recognition, admiration, and a shiny spiritual aura! The daily practice for a would-be mystic involves letting go of resentment and healing the toxicity that is created by it. These are some of the lower-consciousness vibrations that are preventing the progress of spiritual development. Logic and ego continually try to block the intuition and the inner voice of your divine powers. If you are able to let go of the rivalry that the ego creates, you may then be able to swallow such things as pride. Then you may open a door towards creating workable solutions instead. The heart must be opened in order for your past wounds to finally heal. If not, holding on to energies such as grievance and guilt will continue to re-open and create more wounds. This only serves to feed the appetite of the victim – *now is the time to get over it!*

The underworld is a negative dark place where dark forces are held. There are many levels of darkness and evil to be found in the underworld. When a soul finds itself in this environment it is as if that energy is kept in a prism. This often happens without you realising it or even knowing that you are actually there. I will share a couple of personal experiences regarding my journey to the underworld in an effort to gain deeper insight and knowledge.

At an early point in my development I had heard of the underworld and I wanted to visit it to try and help anyone who wanted help. In a meditation I asked my main guide to take me there on a rescue mission. My guide advised me against this as he felt that I would not be heard by those who were there. In his words, "They usually reject any help from the light". I insisted on taking this journey and went deeper into the meditation. My guide and I transcendentally travelled towards the underworld.

I found myself standing in what seemed to be an old village. The village was made up of wooden shanty-like houses. There was a dusty road running through the middle. My guide and I were walking towards the centre of the village when I suddenly stopped outside a buckled wooden house. I noticed that the surrounding wooden fence was also in need of some serious repair work. There was a half-open wooden gate that was leaning to one side due to a missing top hinge. On approaching the house I noticed that there were dirty linen curtains across each of the windows on either side of the door. I looked back at my guide, who stood outside the broken fence and said, "I want to knock on the door." He simply gestured with his hand for me to move forward. I walked further along the broken path towards the door and knocked on the door twice with positive force. Nothing happened. Once again I turned my head to look at my guide as if to ask for help. He remained neutral. I knocked again, this time with a bit more power. Nothing happened for a while and then, there came a croaky voice that said, "Who's there?"

I replied, "I have come to help."

"Go away."

I waited for a moment or two and knocked again. This time I heard footsteps approaching the door. I stepped back as the door began to slowly open with a creaking noise. It stopped opening when the gap was about twenty centimetres wide. I saw an eye, a dirty nose and part of a mouth that showed tarnished teeth as the light made its way through the darkness. I could tell that it was an old man, who was leaning over the gap in the door to look out at me.

"What do you want?" he said in an irritated, strong voice.

"I have come to help heal you and to take you back into the light."

"Go away, I don't want help from you or anyone else," was his reply as he promptly shut the door with a bang, followed by some falling dust.

I stood there for a moment reflecting on my decision to come here. I turned around and looked at my guide; he shrugged his shoulders as if to say, *there is no more you can do*. I made my way back to where he stood waiting patiently by the road. He could see that I was disappointed in my well-intended meaning to help. He turned to me and said, "You may now understand that some do not want help, as bad or as difficult as that may seem to you."

I then truly understood his words of wisdom. But the question still remained in my mind, why did the old man not come to the light with us? My guide picked up on my thoughts and said, "He may not have been ready to take that step. Maybe he needs to go deeper into his hermit-type life before he seeks the light?"

These were comforting and reassuring words for me. I now realise that I could only offer to help. I am not here to preach or persuade anyone to change one way or the other. As an individual I can give an opportunity and if it is not received I must accept that choice. It was a good day for learning.

Here is another example of how help can be offered to another, but is at times not accepted. I was treating a person for alcohol and drug abuse. The individual was living on the earth but in a kind of twilight zone where most physical activity takes place during the night. The individual was a drug pusher as well as a user. He liked to wheel and deal in other areas of life too. He was always looking for an opportunity to make more money. This individual was a bit of a Jack the lad. He came to me seeking help to overcome his addictions and leave the lifestyle he led; he told me that he wanted to change. I first gave him hands-on healing in order to tune into his psyche as a means of finding out what his soul vibration was telling me. Within minutes of this first healing, I was taken back into a scene where I found myself standing in the middle of a square in an old harbour town. It seemed to be somewhere in the south of England during the sixteenth century. It was a dark stormy night and the rain was falling heavily on my head and shoulders. There were a number of streets that entered the town square that were empty. Then I heard some voices just behind me. I turned around and looking through the rain across the wet cobblestones of the square. I was focused on the old oak door of an inn that stood half open. I noticed that above the door there hung a sign saying *The Mackerel and Sprat.* I began walking towards the inn and upon opening the door, a strong wave of energy met me. The smell of human activity and the smoke that accompanied it hit me in the face as I stood there for a few moments. I entered the room; it was a hive of activity. Very few people took note of me as they seemed totally engrossed in their pursuits of drinking and merriment. I moved across the crowded room and stood close to the bar which was fully occupied. I noticed that my patient was sitting down with others around a table. The room was dimly lit and was full of people in various states of intoxication. Most of the souls who were there seemed to be sailors; others were wearing gentlemanly type clothes. There were two buxom bar ladies carrying pewter jugs of beer, they seemed pressed to get on with their work and rushed by due to the handy interference they often encountered from the men. One of the bar ladies laid a jug of beer next to my patient and took one of the many coins that lay next to his cards. The room was humid with the kind of familiar human animal smells that I had encountered before. My patient was fully focused on his gambling affairs with a group of other like-minded characters. The whole atmosphere within this pub was dark, but I felt that there was a real comradeship amongst them, as in a sharing of like-mindedness. I knew that this feeling of comradeship could only be understood by anyone if they had ever worked or been with a team who shared a common goal. The scene was one of drunken disorder, whilst at the same time there was a certain amount of respect for each other. It looked as if my patient was having a good time in his chosen environment. He felt my presence behind him but chose not to engage with me. I could not persuade him to come out of there; he was deeply involved with the gambling and his ego-self had a certain respect from others. This seemed to empower him.

Soon after that the healing came to an end as his soul decided to return. We both regained our presence in the twenty-first century. I explained what I had experienced and seen during the healing. He confirmed certain parts of his experience to me. I said to him "It looks as if you are not yet ready for the change you thought you could make. It seems that your ego still wished to follow the old ways; it has a strong hold over you. If you really want to change, you have to break this addiction to the ego's needs and the power you feel it gives you. If not, it could well end up killing you."

He took this in for some moments before saying, "I will make the change!" He then thanked me for the insight and left. I have not seen him since.

These are but two examples of how the dark side can take over the psyche and keep it in old cycles by recreating them time after time, until that is, a real shift of consciousness comes to the individual. Old habits can be very hard to break as the dark side can hold you in such illusions. It is true to say that emotions and feelings are carried from one lifetime into another. The examples given demonstrate that anyone could find themselves to be caught in a time warp if they are unable to transform their fears. This leads to a very intriguing but old question of which is the real world? Is reality what we make it? And is the underworld such a place of illusions? In my personal experience, I seek to be present in whatever I am doing. I therefore maximise the experiences to their fullest potential through my light body. At other times I may wish to travel to other dimensions to maximise that time in an effort to gain wisdom from higher realms.

If there is a prime motivating factor to raise consciousness on your spiritual journey, it is important to clear any influences that the ego may have over you. These can be the vibrations of doubt, fear, lack of trust, emotional imbalance and lower-mind intervention such as judging another, which can be influential in blocking your higher-soul vibration. The inner transformational work of turning negative energies into positive ones is an important step for any human being to take.

Chapter 9

Possession

In today's climate of consciousness rising, possession is of major concern because it is on the increase due to the general deterioration of the human consciousness through fear. Possession has a number of manifestations. For example there is the physical level where you can be possessed by your own feelings, either towards an object, like desiring a certain car, house or person. Desire has replaced our natural feelings to love unconditionally because the physical need to have has become a stronger force for many. It is also true to say that you can become possessed by another person's thought projections. For example, if I was constantly thinking of you, you would (on some energy level) feel my thoughts, meaning that the former is self-perpetuating. By their very nature, desire and need are prone to the shadow or darker influences because they have the ability to grow into something much bigger if those desires are not fulfilled. This is why corruption has become endemic in societies. To feel rejected on any level is a common phenomenon in this materialistic world and for many, money is power.

An example of a desirer: let us say that you desire another person but that person feels the opposite about you. That person then develops a relationship with another person who is close to you. You become angry because your desire was so strong for that person. You feel rejected because you took it personally and as such did not respect that person's choice. Then your emotions get caught up in the situation and jealousy may pop out of nowhere! You may find it difficult to deal with jealousy and the anger becomes stronger within. The anger can even become violent, as is often the case with jealousy. In this situation the desire became an emotional need which developed into jealousy. Jealousy is an energy that is accepted in all cultures. Desire is not the human being's true nature but we have become attached to it. To the lower mind, all needs are a natural way of life. They appear to be on the outside because that is how the ego works its illusions, which bring a strong desire to be fulfilled. The temporary illusions that desire and need create are traps that restrict the soul's expression to love unconditionally.

An example of a need: have you ever wanted something so badly that you would do almost anything to get it, but when you got it the desire was temporarily fulfilled? If this is the case, then the need for more will always rise as soon as the temporary fulfilment has abated - and what then? Materialistically speaking, you may want a bigger and better car or a house that is out of your reach financially. Many have resorted to criminal actions to fulfil those needs, often to their regret.

These are what I term *lower forms of possession,* which basically consist of one's own emotions that are often projected onto others. All needs can be transformed through discovering and using the tools that are there in your spiritual awakening, such as accepting.

The stronger forms of possession are dark forces that seek to control the psyche of human beings. Possession is a negative force that continually seeks to empower itself through creating fear to control - an example of such a force is a poltergeist. If a way is found by a poltergeist to enter the energy of an individual it can override the lower consciousness to control the senses of that person.

Animal possession: in my experiences of working with possession, I have seen that animal possession usually occurs for the reason of *gaining entry* into the house or dwelling. This may have nothing to do with the occupants of the house, but at the same time it may. Let me make it clearer by giving you two examples through my own experience of how a dark force had gained entry into a house. The two forms of possession explained here are related to dogs. From my own spiritual perspective dogs represent unconditional love. This, I believe, is one of the reasons why a dark force uses (possesses) an animal such as a dog to enter a dwelling in order to create disturbance.

Example 1: the uninvited possession of a dog, I received a phone call one evening from a lady who sounded very disturbed. She informed me that she was having strong disturbances in her house. Objects were moving around in the house by themselves, and at times she heard loud sounds, such as banging, on the floors upstairs. She stated that these disturbances had become stronger in the last two weeks and it had reached a point where it had become very frightening. I made the earliest possible appointment to see her at 11:30 the following day. Before putting the phone down I explained to her that the energy now knew of my coming, and that she should remain focused on the light within her as a form of protection. I also sent my positive light thoughts to the house and her as a form of protection until I was able to physically be there.

I arrived on time the following morning on the front door of the house, which was an attached cottage in a terrace. I knocked on the door and immediately heard the sound of two dogs barking. The front door of the house was of a stable door type split into two. The top part opened and I was kindly greeted by a middle-aged woman. Standing beside her were two German shepherd dogs, and I could tell that one was much older than the other. Before I entered the house I asked the lady to put the dogs in a room, somewhere where they would not disturb us. She promptly led them to an upstairs room, but they continued to bark. I then entered the small house that consisted of one large downstairs room behind which was a small kitchen and a bathroom. A wooden stairway led upstairs, where I was told that there were three small bedrooms.

From where I stood in the middle of the living room, I could feel certain negative forces. I requested to investigate further and was told by the owner that I could do so. After assessing the small kitchen, bathroom and larger living room downstairs I made my way up the stairs. On the landing immediately to my left was the room where the dogs were locked up. They were still barking loudly, particularly the young one. I looked into the partly opened door that led into a bedroom directly in front of me, but felt no strong negative energies emanating from there. I then turned to my right and entered what seemed to be the main bedroom. There was a small window that overlooked the valley in front of the house. On entering the room I immediately felt a chill falling all over my entire body. I said to myself, *There is definitely a strong negative force in this room.* I also knew that this was a room in which there was an entrance point. Almost all houses that are possessed by stronger forces (such as poltergeists) create an entrance point, which is more commonly known as a "portal". (Yes, it is a bit like a *Star Gate* portal.) In this room I could see that the portal was directly at the site of the window. I could see that it was a strong one because it was so clear. I immediately went back downstairs to inform the owner that I was ready to begin the deeper work of clearing the house of all negative forces.

In my shoulder bag I had already brought the necessary tools with me, ones that I had been guided to bring to support the exorcism. I picked up the bag and instructed the owner to sit down by the open fire and to focus on the candlelight and to try and remain peaceful within. I advised her to continue focusing on the light. I then began to make my way back up the stairs. I could hear one of the dogs scratching violently on the door with its claws in an effort to get at me. I entered the main bedroom where the portal was. I put a chair that was already in the room some two metres in front of the window and portal. I had my glass of water and a candle by my side. I took a sip of water and looked into the candle light for a moment before focusing my attention back on the portal. I went into my usual meditative state in order to get in touch on a deeper level with the portal and its creator. The view of what was there came to me almost immediately as I opened my psyche in order to enter its vibration. As I connected to the negative force, it became obvious that I was now facing a very strong energy. I also understood that the energy was not even of this dimension (universe). Then a force appeared all around me and began to attack me in an effort to destroy me. I held my place and stayed anchored in the light, not fearing anything. The negative alien force approached and attacked me by pressurising me three times, and each time it gained strength. The third time was the strongest; it literally tried to squeeze everything out of me. But after the third attempt it became weaker as the light within me became stronger. The negative energy then decided to escape and it went through the portal in an attempt to escape my presence. The only thing I can say at this point is, ***There is no hiding place in the universe for any dark force.*** After I had spent some moments pursuing this negative force I duly transformed the energy, closed the portal and sealed it so that return was not possible. Then I could feel that there was peace once more in the house. During this time dealing with the alien energy I had also been focusing on the owner and both dogs with healing, and they were also cleared of the negative forces that had been present.

I went back down the stairs (noticing that the dogs were now a bit quieter) to rejoin the owner. I had informed the lady that all was now well again and that she could sleep in peace once more. I did not go into greater detail of what I had dealt with, but I will say that it was also an initiation for me. Three days later I was shopping in the local town when I bumped into the lady of this house. She immediately told me that the house felt so good now - peaceful was the word! She then said, "But do you know, after you had left I brought the dogs downstairs again. After about thirty minutes the young dog got up and started to turn in a circle in the middle of the living room, like he was making a nest. The dog then lay down and died before my very eyes." I then asked her, "Where did you get the dog from?" and she replied "From a dog's home just up the road."I asked her how old it was and she answered, "Only eighteen months."

I then understood that the dog had also been possessed and that after my healing and transformational work to remove the evil energy, the physical presence of the dog no longer served the purpose of the dark force because its life supply had been cut off during the exorcism. However I must strongly stress that this form of possession with dogs is by no means a common phenomena, it is a very, very rare occurrence.

Example 2: I was invited to attend a Saturday night party by some recent acquaintances. At approximately ten o'clock I duly went along to their apartment. On ringing the bell the door was opened. I could hear and feel the party was in full swing and on entering the main living room I immediately got a fuller picture of the energies present. The room was full of cigarette smoke and there was much alcohol of various types on offer. I made contact with the party throwers and others that I already knew from the local community. Quite central to the room was a large coffee table on which was laid some items of food and soft drinks. I duly helped myself to a soft drink and then got into a conversation with others. I noticed that the owners had a small black dog (Scottish terrier type) that was walking around and sniffing everyone. As the evening went on I noticed that many in the room were smoking hash or marijuana. Some were sitting alone in their own world, isolated, doing their own thing. By one o'clock in the morning there were only three people (me included) who were sober and clear-minded enough to have a good conversation, bearing in mind that I have the ability to block the effects of the smoke from this soft drug (as it is now described). I sat down for some moments when the dog came over to me. It approached in a cautious manner. The dog held its head high to try and get a better sense of me. I noticed that its face seemed to be distorted or certainly out of character for its type of breeding. I then went to touch the dog over its head, but was immediately challenged as it tried to bite me. I then saw that the dog was possessed. The dog moved away from me looking back as it did so. I watched it going around the room acting curious towards other people. Some fifteen minutes later the dog came back towards me. It was hungry and looking for food. On the table was a bowl of small meatballs, and these meatballs seemed very attractive to the dog. Then, acting on an unconscious level, I picked up one of the meatballs and offered it to the dog. The dog came closer (but was still wary of me) and closer, lifting its nose into the air to connect to the smell of the meat ball. The dog now stood some distance away from my right hand which contained the meatball. I could feel the dog's greed for food and at that moment the dog went to grab the meatball that lay in my outstretched hand. As it did I filled the meatball with light. The dog gulped the meatball in an effort to swallow it but struggled for a moment to do so; it was choking in its effort to swallow. The meatball was then swallowed and went down into the stomach. I knew that a healing had taken place. The next day I returned to collect something that I had forgotten. When the door was opened this happy dog came running up to greet me. I duly picked it up and saw how beautiful it looked, it had returned to its natural looks and was clear of any dark force.

In this example, the owners of the dog may have not been responsible for it being possessed. Dark spirits can do what I term "jump" from one energy form to another, be it from animal to human or vice versa. In this example I would say that the possession was due to the negative activities of those smoking soft drugs that were responsible for the dog's possession. This gives me an opportunity to explain, from my experience, how drugs can have such a negative effect upon the psyche in a way that can leave you open to possession.

Drugs and their effects: hashish – marijuana – heroin – cocaine and alcohol.

Whenever anyone uses any of the drugs listed above there are certain simulative effects to be considered and recognise as being dangerous and harmful for mind, body and spirit. One of these is the over stimulation of *dopamine*. Let us look briefly into the effects of dopamine before pursuing the possibility of being possessed whilst under the influences of soft and hard drugs alike. But firstly it is important to state that narcotics are mentally orientated, and due to this fact are the most dangerous in terms of possible possession; whilst alcohol is emotionally based. Those who consume much alcohol are of little or no importance to a dark force such as a poltergeist. This is due to the fact that the mind (lower consciousness) of an individual is a main point of entry for possession and not the emotional body.

Some insight: the above drugs are responsible for the release or over-release of dopamine. Dopamine is the neurone transmitter that runs the motivation and reward systems within all human beings. This neurotransmitter increases our anticipation of happiness and as such make the user want more of the thing that provides them with that rush of happiness.

The feelings that arise from so-called[45] "soft drugs" are often felt as being pleasant and happy, which only makes the user seek the sensation again and again. This can create an addiction and the individual will seek to engage more strongly in the behaviour and use of the drugs that cause dopamine to be released.

---

45 There is very little awareness of the dangers involved in all forms of simulative drugs, the likes of which are mentioned here.

Although dopamine essentially directs desire, the actual feeling of pleasure comes from endorphins. Endorphin is a substance produced by the brain and the pituitary gland; it contains pain-killing properties similar to morphine.

There is much that you may read into the above facts - which I am sure you will peruse in your own particular way to help you to become more clear of the dangers of drug use and abuse!

It is wise to remember that all forms of addiction require abstinence from a drug for a minimum of *ninety days* to render a possible cure. According to scientific material, if an individual abstains for *eighty-five days, this is not enough.* They must have the full ninety days. This is due to a chemical change that occurs in the area of the brain that is affected by the addictive properties of the drug, which only changes after a *ninety day* period of abstinence. *This period of healing is also true for other addictions, like coffee!*

With all drug takers, there is an underlying need which is chiefly mentally based. It is an act of escaping - be it for a moment or hours. Drugs such as *marijuana hashish, heroin and cocaine* carry a cocktail of chemicals that have a definite negative effect upon the lower mental body and the emotions. However, what is equally as important to recognise is the effect these drugs have upon the psyche and higher consciousness. There are a couple of things simultaneously happening here that I feel should be made clearer:

1: *The drug itself:* the quality or purity of the drug itself determines its effect upon the user's physiological and psychic abilities. For example, with a drug such as cocaine, there have been countless reports of this drug being laced with other (chemical) substances that are definitely a danger to life. Human greed, which is a dark force, is a real issue here for those who are into dealing in such narcotics. The ego and the shadow dominate the lives of those who deal in this increasing negative supply of narcotics, and many dealers are users themselves. They are trapped by their own addiction and so must sell more to pay for their addiction.

2: *The human psyche:* each individual is a chemical factory that produces the required chemistry in order to keep the physical body functioning normally. This aspect in relation to narcotics is inevitably linked firstly to *the drug itself,* because the same chemistry of the drug will have a different effect (which could be small or big) upon the individual concerned. A friend of yours may say to you, *"Here, take some of this, it is a great experience."* If you choose to take the drug you will have an experience that may be totally different to that of your friend, simply because you are not that person; your inner chemistry is different.

A drug may have some seemingly pleasurable effects on the physical aspect of you, but what about the psyche or higher self? It is often believed that by taking soft drugs such as hashish and marijuana you will find it easier to meditate. My understanding of this is quite the opposite, not only is it an illusion but is dangerous. But let us first ask the question - why take any drugs at all to have a spiritual experience? The answer to this may perhaps lie in the brief explanation of the effects that dopamine has on the physical body and mind therein. From my perspective, the bottom line is that if there is a need or desire for any form of artificial stimulation in your life and indeed regarding your spiritual practice; there must be a lack of self-love within.

Meditation and soft drugs: some choose a path of combining drugs and sometimes alcohol with their spiritual path. My insight and experience of this is that it is not possible to obtain clarity of mind or body whilst under the influence of either soft drugs or alcohol. Here's why. Certain drugs (not alcohol) are known to have the effect of opening higher consciousness towards visualising realms beyond the physical or experiencing other dimensions, such as alien beings or nature spirits. This can be a strong incentive for an individual to try a certain drug with the aim of experiencing what is called *an altered state of consciousness* during meditation. In a physical sense, the words "altered state of consciousness" may be true, but esoterically speaking they are not. The drugs affect two or more levels of consciousness and not just the singular logic, 3D. The main reason being that the drug itself is an artificial stimulus; this may open the psyche to an experience whilst perusing a meditation. Because the experience (whilst under the influence of the drug) is not a natural stimulation of the 3D into the 4D, there are dangers involved, such as possible possession by a dark force.

The drug actually clouds the consciousness of higher mind orientation due to its chemical input. I see it like steering your ship in the fog, where you do not know where you are going or what is coming to you. You have no radar because your intuition is blocked. In other words you are not in control, the drug and its influences are! Equally important to mention here is that the experience is not truly registered in the mental body as an esoteric experience of a journey, thereby making it invalid as a spiritual experience.

Meditation gives you an opportunity to clear your mind and body as a means to access and develop your higher senses, those of clairvoyance, clairaudience and clairsentience. This is on the whole done naturally by stimulating the body's chemistry through focusing your consciousness inwardly towards oneness, that of self love. The light you attract activates your higher senses by drawing more light into the pineal and pituitary glands in the head, which are termed esoterically "seats of higher consciousness". These glands are chiefly responsible for opening the higher consciousness that is connected to your entire chakra system, which in turn governs the entire lymphatic system. This does not happen when the individual is inducing chemical change through narcotics in order to obtain an altered state of mind.

The method of *"creative visualisation meditation"* **follows three basic steps**

Step one: firstly direct the lower-mind point of focus towards being open to all possibilities. Imagination does this in a subtle manner by allowing the lower mind to follow a directive that is given to it in a creative manner; such as imagining that you are on a beach or standing on a mountain top. The lower mind's imagination would take you to a beach or a mountain top because you have been to either or both and experienced them before. The lower mind will imagine it and you will see it clearly through your picture memory because it trusts where that place is, simply because it knows it to be safe from a past experience.

Step two: this step is to take the consciousness into the creative mode (a step above logic). This essentially means that you discover your beach in a new manner, because your mind is crossing or rising into your higher consciousness exceptional view.

Step three: here you are two steps away from logical control and are able to perceive what is on your beach. You may see and feel what the ocean and sky looks like or what may come to you (as a form of guidance) from either, such as a dolphin or a bird. When you are in this third step of perception, your higher consciousness is open to receive universal guidance, whilst at the same time being grounded in your body. From this perspective within the meditation, the reality of the meditation becomes established within yourself. What you perceive in your meditation goes beyond the limited perception of logic. The meditation helps logic to cross over into higher consciousness, aiding what is being experienced to become more concrete to the logical mind. An essential tool that you can use during your creative visualisation meditation is the law of demand. This law essentially means that you have the right to ask universal consciousness questions of what may come to you during a meditation. If, for example, a dolphin appears you may wish to join the dolphin in the ocean and to ask why it has come to you. Without asking you may sit there for a thousand years and not receive any guidance. Perception and a healthy sense of curiosity help to open the three higher senses, which is a major step towards becoming self-realisation. It is important to ask in order to receive - how else can the universe respond to your thoughts?

When these three steps are followed during your meditation, the light of higher consciousness will naturally follow its flow as long as the logical chit chat within the lower mind has been managed. The chemistry within the physical self is naturally produced to give you every opportunity to access the higher-self in meditation. This allows the experience to be registered within your own physical self and felt by the senses. The experience can be uplifting and not confusing to all levels of consciousness. You will also be able to return to the same place you experienced on your meditational journey. This is due to the fact that you will have established an awareness of higher perception from within your spiritual eye to the visual cortex. You will also hold the light that came with it, and use its power to move you forward in your meditational practice.

Every human being has the ability to meditate in this manner. Meditation is a key towards your enlightenment. It has endless uses because it allows your higher self to explore your life's journey without the interference of the lower mind. The lower mind does not have the tools and know-how to meditate, but at the same time, takes its place in the important step of accepting what may appear in order to explore further.

The left hemisphere of the brain does not require any form of drug to reach an altered state of mind. What is required is a rewiring of logic to the right hemisphere which contains higher mind principles. The right hemisphere has the ability to perceive energies and forces that are to be found beyond the limits of the physical realm, that of the paranormal. It is important to understand that there are certain energies that emanate from the lower mind that continually seek to dominate your thoughts and feelings in an attempt to control, and one method of control is using fear to keep you away from meditation.

The mentally ill and possession: this is an area where I have had some strong experiences of treating others as a therapist. I believe that there are deep levels of ignorance and misgivings in regards to how the mentally ill are both treated and institutionalised. I believe the words "imbalanced or having a lack of harmony" are more descriptive when considering the mentally ill. Imbalance for me indicates that a chemical exchange has taken place in the consciousness of a mentally imbalanced person. For example, the start of the imbalance could possibly be traced back to a strong emotional event in that person's life. There could have been great trauma attached to the event. Such a moment can influence the mental body (lower mind) and its conscious choices in a negative manner. Lack of harmony for me is representative of the individual being separated from their divine vibration, that of love. It is indeed a vast field to be working in which has many specialised areas. But I would like to give some insights in three aspects that may shed some light for psychologists, psychiatrists and doctors who are working in this area.

1: Schizophrenia and psychosis (Tardive):[46] in my experience of treating patients with psychic disorders they usually have strong hallucinations, which are often connected to the paranormal. An example of this is that the person sees spirit forms or hears voices that appear to be coming from outside of themselves. For this to occur (literally speaking) the patient must have in some way opened their higher senses, those of clairaudience and clairsentience, in order to experience what they are truly seeing, hearing and feeling.

Because of the lack of awareness, insight or even training by the medical profession in the energy of the paranormal and their life forces, I believe great ignorance remains, which is something that the patient has to deal with. The logical training of professions, such as standard psychology, does not and cannot enter the area of higher-mind principles by logic alone. There is a rela-

46 Tardive psychosis is a form of psychosis distinct from schizophrenia and induced by the use of current (dopaminergic) antipsychotics by the depletion of dopamine and related to the known side effect caused by their long-term use e.g. Tardive dyskinesia

tive understanding of logical thinking - 3D conscious-ness – that is relevant to the five physical senses. The fourth and fifth-dimensional consciousnesses (4D-5D) are present in all beings, but not recognised by the sci-ences, which is unfortunate to say the least. I feel that the complete essence of life[47] is not being fully investigated or considered. The human being is orientated through higher consciousness and not the other way around i.e. logic to higher consciousness. Higher consciousness is the guiding principle to the life force which is not yet recognised by many in the relative sciences. It is quite clear for me that the logic cannot be the creator of the physical self - the spirit and soul are. Logic is designed to help co-ordinate the physical senses that are linked to the material world. It is good at achieving, but beyond the limitations of the 3D consciousness (time, distance and matter, cause and effect) it is unable to fully compre-hend such fields as quantum physics without the active presence (be it limited thus far) of higher consciousness.

I am basically stating that logic does not have the insight or tools with which to treat those who experience the paranormal in the manner described here. Other than treating the imbalance with strong anti-psychotic drugs (which often create the very symptoms they are meant to prevent) there seems to be no magic pill or solution that both transforms a possessed individual as well as treating those who hear alien voices.

From my experience I believe that the patient who states that they are hearing voices or seeing other beings, to a great degree is. Yes they are real! But due to the lack of insight, belief or training of the medical profession, patients that demonstrate such signs are often labelled as being either *schizophrenic or psychotic*, and are duly treat-

---

47 Spirit and soul energies. Spirit motivates the body and the Soul has cre-ated it. Both provide the experience of life lived through body consciousness.

ed as such. When a person is at this level of imbalance (hearing and seeing forces or energies outside or inside of themselves) they are not lost by any means. It is possible to restore a balanced mental body by using holistic methods that recognise or even witness the presence of an alien force that is interfering with the patient's mental state. With the use of one's higher senses, the clairvoyance and clairaudient faculties will provide real insight into the alien energies and much can be accomplished. Through holistic methods of healing, such as hands-on healing, such imbalances can be treated by exhuming the alien energies by exorcism, and thus restoring good health in mind, body, spirit and soul.

It is important to recognise that individually we contain a unique chemical fingerprint, and as such must be treated on that basis. In my opinion there is a great need to correctly train staff how to deal with possession. When implemented, there will in the long run, be less patients admitted into mental institutions due to possession. The opposite (which is very much the norm) is that patients are treated or blanket-fed with drugs that predictably suppress the symptoms and don't treat the cause. However those prescribing the drugs do not take into account individualism, which for me is a tragedy for the patient. When a patent is given a drug for the above imbalances, the body and psyche of the individual must first adjust to the effects of the drug. The negative effects are termed "side effects". At this experimental stage (and there are many), any number of drugs may be given over a period of days, weeks or even months, to ascertain which one or ones are deemed to be most suited to the patient's condition of mind and body. All anti-psychotic drugs numb the natural feelings by blocking certain receptors to the brain. These are meant to change or transform the state of consciousness experienced by the patient. This may be true to a degree. Because their mental state has not changed, the way in which the mental body deals with the chemical input changes their actions.

What of the natural feelings and the senses that are so intertwined with the patient? I have experiences of being with patients who have become so numbed by medication that they have become what I term "zombiefied". When the patient is in this state they are not even able to fight or restore the imbalance because they are not in touch with their core senses and feelings. The chemistry of the drugs prescribed to the individual changes their own body chemistry due to the artificial input and control it has over their psyche. I know that the word "alien" may seem a bit strong here, but for me, anti-psychotic drugs are just that. I see this form of treatment as a slippery road to a long-lasting state of imbalance, partly because the patient is unable to comprehend normal consciousness in order to help restore their own health.

It is also important to note that when an individual hears an alien voice, the force may not have truly entered their energy fields or psyche, as is the case with a fully possessed person. Therefore from my perspective, alien energies that are interfering and creating a certain amount of imbalance by accessing the consciousness of the individual, can be treated and cleared from interfering or entering the mental body of the individual. This is possible by helping them to restore their normal sense of mental orientation. I must also state that this is (to a great degree) only possible if the patient has not received any form of medical drugs. Such drugs only serve to block the healer's path from entering the patient's consciousness, and make it more difficult to remove an alien force.

2: *The possessed:* with this type of imbalance, individual experiences are quite different from the outer experiences described above. However, the possessed may demonstrate some symptoms of schizophrenia and psychosis. With the possessed patient, the alien force (darkness) has actually gained access into the physical temple, or mind. Access by the alien force occurs chiefly through the lower mental body (logic or mind), unless that is, the person has an overactive emotional body (third chakra) or an over-stimulated sacral (second chakra) or sexually-orientated energy. But the latter, emotional and sacral aspects are seldom entrance points for dark forces.

As mentioned earlier in this book, the use of narcotics is a cause of possession. This is also true for those who work with negative spiritual practices, as is often the case when an individual or group work with occult black magic. The depth of possession is chiefly determined by the strength or level of intelligence of the alien's energy that is attracted by certain rituals. I have treated people who have been possessed by two or more dark energies. However this is not a common event. All dark forces are there for one reason only - to control. From the outset any dark force seeks to control the life principle of the whole physical body in an attempt to control the spirit and soul. One main route is through the lower mind by creating fear, in order to control.

A common way in which a dark force seeks to enter an individual (when not yet within) is to make all kinds of promises to that person. It will say to the individual "I am from the light, follow my guidance and I will help you". Or it may well seek to guide by telling you what the future is or who is doing what, when and where. This may impress the one receiving these insights and messages through the higher faculties of their higher senses. But as is usual with all forms of evil, there comes *payback time.* The payback for a dark force is to make the individual do something that is against their normal behaviour. This could be as simple as being nasty to someone - revenge being the force. In this manner the dark force tries to break the contact that the individual has with their higher consciousness, that of love and light. How deep the possession is determines how strong a connection they have to their higher senses, whether they are seeing clearly, and how much control it has over the rational as it continually seeks to get it its own way.

It is my strong belief that many crimes are committed by possessed people. This means that it is not the individuals themselves who are directly responsible for their actions, but the dark force or forces within.

Dark forces have one purpose, that is to control and destroy all light forces such as good hearted people, servers of the greater good. Many murders and assassinations are enacted because the dark force has possessed the individual and the individual may not even be aware of what they are doing in those moments. It could be termed a form of madness whenever such a crime is looked at purely from the logic, but in these situations I can tell you it is often far from being black or white. All dark forces of this nature are intelligent and powerful. They are organised enough to destroy a light worker, often indirectly. If you look at how many politicians have been assassinated in the twenty-first century, you begin to get the bigger picture of the intent behind all dark and evil forces. Yes, the evil is there and it uses others to do its work through possession. It is up to each and every one of us to end its presence. For that to happen, the greater majority of the world's population must work for the light from within themselves by transforming the ego, fear and emotional aspects of their human nature.

3: *The split personality:* an individual that is known to have a split personality, as the word suggests, seemingly holds two identities. The personalities in this instance are not those of the higher and lower nature, logic and soul. The person may be motivated through their emotions or their ego which may contain elements of darkness and evil. These are elements that are often hidden and controlled by the essence of pure logic. For ease of reference I shall call them aspect A and aspect B.

Aspect A: emotional imbalance. This person may be kind, considerate and caring over long periods of time (days, weeks or months). But during this period, something may trigger a negative aspect that rises to the surface where it can be seen. For example this aspect is one of jealousy. Jealousy can split the person from being kind in one moment, to being accusing, cruel and even violent in the next. Jealousy is indeed a dark force which has strong roots connected to deep emotional imbalance. Jealousy has deep controlling issues due to a lack of self-worth. Whenever the dark force of jealousy arises within an individual, it is usually accompanied by a deep-seated anger; the anger can become so strong that all rational thinking goes out through the window as the emotional aspects of it gains in power. It can become uncontrollable and violent! If a person is following such a behaviour pattern and behaves in a strong and violent manner, at the end of an outburst they usually feel deep remorse and can be apologetic. They may have realised their weakness and seek forgiveness - which I believe is a step in the right direction. However, be aware and do not be fooled by such behaviour. Jealousy is actually seeking attention but at the same time it can turn and destroy.

The personality of a jealous person is deeply controlling and when that does not work or seems not to work, it may rise like a demon from nowhere! Deep-seated jealousy requires healing and transformation from within the jealous person; it cannot be done from the outside i.e. by another person. This is often attempted in the belief that by continuing to make it right for that person or pleasing them, their behaviour pattern will change. This is an illusion; continuing to make it right for the jealous individual simply feeds the jealousy, nothing changes on a deeper level. Do not be fooled! You cannot directly change a person, they have to change themselves.

Aspect B: Ego's control. The ego is created by incorrect use of mind and emotion. Some of the elements that support the ego's directive are fear and more fear. When trust and faith are not present in your life, fear often is. The ego's identity is based upon its needs, desires and judgement. The former two feed it and the latter creates the separation that helps to give it identity and meaning - a direction in which to move.

Another major factor that the ego plays with is control. It always seeks to control its environment because it fears to fail in any respect. All of these build up into a body of energy that is an illusion of emotions and mind. Yes, it is self-created and self-perpetuating. It is the negative dark force that is responsible for much of the darkness that touches everyone on some level. It is impossible to truly love when ego is ruling your life. You may feel that you are having a loving moment or caring for someone, but what is the consciousness behind your way of being, are you true to your feelings or are you looking for a reward of some kind? For example, are you emotionally connected or do you feel more deeply for what you are experiencing? Is your connection with another emotionally based or is it unconditional love? The ego will even convince you that you are important and should be noticed, because the ego continually seeks positive feedback about itself. It fears any form of rejection and will do anything to prevent that from happening, which is why the ego continually tries to keep your thoughts in the past or future, and often both at the same time. This is the ego's way to keep re-manifesting your fears in order to control your actions. I personally view the ego as the shadow side of the self, because it continually keeps on stepping in front to block your way. Confusion and doubt are a few examples of the ego at work.

All dark and evil forces are aspects of the human consciousness that have chosen to step away from the light of truth, love and joy. Everyone who has experienced dark and evil in whatever manner will instinctively understand this. Every human being that reincarnates is given equal opportunity to transform any negativity that they may hold in their psyche. The only reason anyone reincarnates is to return to their original state of divine light, a being that holds the qualities of love, peace and joy.

Chapter 10

The Art of Exorcism &
Haunted Places and People

The consciousness of evil is as strong as we make it to be or believe it to be, which, it could be argued is the same thing. So let us step out of fear and enter the light by recognising these truths:

- *To understand the nature of darkness is to understand the truth of light.*

- *To be in the truth you must be free from fear to be in the light.*

- *To walk in the light you must be present.*

Haunted places such as houses, castles and hotels are common phenomena in all countries and continents. Yes this phenomenon is of a global magnitude, and each cultural region and continent employs its own particular style of transforming and healing any negative force. Generally speaking, the energy or energies present in places that are haunted are of the same essence. They are forms of spirit, which in itself contains levels of consciousness, and must be respected. These spirit forms basically appear as Thought-forms, ghosts, ghouls and poltergeists, as well as others which are too deep to mention in this book.

It is important to understand that spirit is all around and that good or bad spirits are everywhere. Spirit forms cannot be seen by the physical eyes unless the spirit wishes to be seen on the physical level. Essentially, spirit forms are vibrating on a higher vibration of light to that of the denser physical body. The energy of a spirit being is referred to as an etheric form and every living person has one. The etheric energy of a ghost is often described as being like a mist or cloudy presence. It is true to say that humans fear mostly what cannot be seen. But that does not necessarily mean that what cannot be seen is a negative thing; the logical mind creates the fear that is inbuilt into your natural protective mechanism. Fear is an illusion that most find difficult to transform because it is well established in the human psyche of their lower nature.

There are both dark and light spirit beings, the only difference between them is that the light spirit being vibrates on a higher plane of consciousness, that of love. What is referred to as a ghost is a spirit that is often lost between worlds. The ghost recognises if a person is able to see it or not. The logic mind that assesses what the physical eyes see is unable to see spirit forms unless the spirit lowers its vibration. This is because the physical eye's view of the world is through physical light that reflects back the denser forms of matter. If a person is able to feel the presence of a spiritual force but is unable to see it, the spiritual force will sometimes lower its vibration in order for it to be seen as a ghostly figure by the physical eyes. The clairvoyant and clairaudient person is however able to both see and connect telepathically with beings of spirit without them lowering their vibration. This is only possible by developing and harmonising the vibration levels (consciousness) of the third eye and visual cortex to receive and register what is seen on the etheric level.

For example, mediums go beyond the normal physical senses by accessing and utilising their higher senses. A key fact to remember here is that everything in existence is created through various forms of light i.e. consciousness. This is explained with deeper insight in some of the more common phenomena listed below:

1: *Negative thought forms* take the least power to clear. They are usually manifested through human emotions which are linked to the common thoughts, logic. All thoughts have energy, and the lower consciousness or 3D is electromagnetic in its nature. Your thoughts travel through the electromagnetic field that surrounds the earth and as such must go somewhere. When our thoughts are (for whatever reason) tainted with anger, revenge or both they can be directed towards an individual. Such projection will instantly reach its target on some level, and will have a definite effect upon that person's psyche. You can put positive or negative thoughts into much of what you do in your everyday living - be it cooking food or being in your workplace. The energy is the same, it must go somewhere. For example, you may be having a bad day at the office and you carry that anger onto the bus or train with you. You sit down and when you leave you will leave that negative imprint on the chair. A total stranger comes on the bus after you have left and sits down on the seat you have just left. How much they pick up of your negative implant depends on their sensitivity. If the individual is energy-aware and present, they person will not choose to sit on the seat you have just left with a negative imprint, but will move to another place that is clear of negative energies.

Everything you personally own (a ring, keys or clothes etc) holds information about you. The implanted thought-energy can be tapped into or read by using the technique of Psychometry. You can confirm the reality of what I am explaining here by giving a reading of a friend's ring, for example - you may then realise how important it is to take care of our thoughts. If you have received a gift that is second hand or you buy something from a second hand shop I would recommend that you clean it as it may be loaded with the previous owner's thoughts and feelings. If you do not clean it or get it cleansed by a person who knows what they are doing (a medium) those very energies may have a negative effect on your psyche. You can cleanse them by simply passing conscious light through them to transform anything negative that may be within. I have on occasions dealt with spirit thought forms which grew in strength due to the fear that it created in the house in which it was present. The reality of the spirit form is in general the same as it is for the physical, though on another level (the etheric level).

2: *Ghosts* hold a higher vibration to that of the thought form energy. Ghosts also appear in a variety of forms and for various reasons. One is that the ghost may be lost in its transition (from one realm to another) which usually occurs soon after physical death. It is usually the case that as your consciousness passes from one dimension to another (earth to heaven) you (the soul within) are met by a guiding light that accompanies you to your home place or world in this your local universe. Sometimes this does not happen for a variety of reasons. One is that the death process was an instant and violent one, such as being run over by a car. When this occurs, the spirit and soul within is in a total state of shock, due to the violence of the accident. The physical body is now lifeless leaving the spirit and soul within, with no home or temple because its life force has been destroyed, i.e. the heart stops beating.

I have experienced ghostly phenomena when I was driving a car on the west coast of Wales. It was late at night, around 11.30 pm. I was driving down a small gully; I could see that the road ahead of me was perfectly clear. I had reached the bottom of the gully and was about to drive up it when in a flash I saw a woman dressed in a brown coat standing in the middle of the road directly in the path of my car. I hit her full on and she rolled over the bonnet towards my driving side and onto the road. I hit the brakes full on (a subconscious act) and screeched to a stop. I jumped out of the car expecting to find a dead body at the side of the road. But there was none, not a drop of blood on the car, not even a mark of dent to be seen. I was very shaken by this experience, but I was more shocked to not find a body; I was totally bemused. The next morning I again checked the car for damage, but found none. I told a close friend of my driving experience the night before. His reply was, "Was it down in that dip by such and such a village?"

"Yes" I said.

"Ah, that will be the girl who is haunting that part of the road, it happens every now and again at that same spot. The young woman was killed by a car in that same place some twenty years ago."

From this experience you may now see the relevance of what I am explaining, but please keep in mind that it is uncommon for those killed in such a way to not pass over.

It is wise to remember that the great majority of those who are journeying back to the **Pearly Gates** do have a clear transition. Usually whenever a place is haunted, the spirit of the person is not able to let go of its earthly possessions, such as a house; their experiences and memory may be too strong for them to let go. This is often due to their attachment, as they may have spent most of their lifetime in such a home or house. When their time comes to return to the original source they are unable to let go of their connections to it; the memories may be too strong. They can remain in the house for long periods of time - decades, even centuries. Ghosts are lost souls that are caught between worlds and are often unaware of this, even on a timescale.

It is also true to say that time in this matter has no real bearing, therefore a century may seem like a day to that particular soul. It is often the case that people hold on to a ghostly figure in their homes, and is even at times exploited by making those places a tourist attraction. To many, the ghost becomes a matter of curiosity, even to the extent where it becomes a fashion figure; this to me is a tragedy. The whole purpose of the healer who works in this area is to release the ghost from its prison in order to direct it back to its original source. On its return it may continue its journey in order to be reabsorbed back into universal consciousness and return to earth in a physical form through universal law of reincarnation. So yes, if you have a ghost that is presently in your dwelling, seek an exorcist to direct the spirit back to its source of light.

3: Ghouls are of the same essence as ghosts but appear in disfigured forms due to their nature. They can also smell quite badly, which is a good indication that a ghoul is there. Ghouls are usually corrupted in some manner and are unable to face themselves, so they focus their attention on others by creating disturbances and playing games with their powers to frighten those of earthly mind.

4: *Poltergeists* - out of all spirit forms, it takes the most power to exhume or clear the energy of a poltergeist from premises. This is mainly due to the high consciousness they hold. They know exactly how to use and direct their forces to maximise their own purposes. The energy of the poltergeist is always about directing its force to control its near-environment, as it would have done on the earth plane whilst the spirit remained in its physical life form. The poltergeist is an extremely negative force that chooses not to return to the light. It appears for a number of reasons, the main reason being to dominate another soul through possessing their body, spirit and soul.

One of the most common ways of entry (into a house or person) for a poltergeist is through it being invited by the ignorance of the caller. The caller in this instance could be an individual or two or more people playing with black magic to invite a force into their group, usually to use its power. This is commonly done by inexperienced people using a ouija board, which is an upturned glass on a table with numbers and the alphabet laid out in a circle ready for the communication. To use this crude method of communicating with a spirit is like the blind being led by the blind where great dangers are present. Of course there is no guarantee that the spirit being called for by the group will be a pure one. But usually one gets what one needs to learn and the reflection is always true to the cause! It is my belief that the majority of those using this method find or tune in to real dark energies.

On a number of occasions I have had to help people or groups of people out of this situation. The vibration of a Ouija board will attract any negative force that is near due to its very nature, i.e. undeveloped beings playing roulette with spirit.

When a poltergeist has gained access into a home it will play the game of firstly creating fear with the occupants of the house. It creates this in order to seek greater control over their psyche, which is easily done, as people in general fear what they do not see or understand. The fear that is generated will only serve to feed the poltergeist's energy, where negativities feed the negative. I have found that it is quite common for a poltergeist to enter a dwelling via those that seek an adventure or wish to play with magic via such devices as a ouija board. This can be a dangerous path to follow. It is a bit like picking up the phone and dialling a random number with the wish that the person on the other end will be a **good guy**. It is a lottery due to the low vibration of psychic energy involved in this kind of experiment. Yes, the blind leading the blind in this case.

The poltergeist is an intelligent dark energy, and as such it will absorb anything that is negative. It will also use negative energy as a tool to create even deeper fears. Unlike the ghost phenomena, the poltergeist chooses to be in a given place, and that place is usually where it will find the least resistance in order to increase its powers.

All poltergeists come from a level of consciousness that I refer to as the *dark belt* which encircles the earth. Poltergeists will seek every opportunity to prematurely return to the earth plane, other than by their karmic path, which includes the natural birth channel and its karmic significance. In this way they disown their responsibility for whatever negativity they may have created in previous lives, and as such seek to disown their karmic debt. They are rogue spirits that have no conscience, love or compassion for other soul beings. They are simply here to create as much negativity as is possible, and will use any means to do that in order to keep their power. I have witnessed such powers writing fearful messages with lipstick on a bathroom mirror. Just as a positive spirit can lift a table to stand on one leg so can a negative spirit learn to throw furniture around a room. That is how physical they can be and often do become.

Powerful poltergeists seek to possess a person to take control over their soul's guidance in order to live their life of darkness through that individual's physical body. The normal route in for the poltergeist is to firstly access the individual's lower mind, the logical aspect, in order to control the soul's will. I have seen many such cases in mental institutions globally. I can see when such individuals are possessed. This phenomenon can be recognised by their displaying such symptoms whereby they hear a voice within their head and often see the entity through the higher mind's eye, or third eye. But tragically in most cases the individual is not listened to on a deeper level by the doctor and psychologist and is labelled as psychologically disturbed or hallucinatory. When in fact in the greater majority of cases, they have an imbalanced mental body[48] that could be restored to normal functioning through correct therapy. The therapy of spiritual healing or hands-on-healing is often very effective in removing a poltergeist, as long as they are treated with healing prior to any medical intervention. Once suppressive drugs have been administered to a person of this nature they will block the very mental neuron transmitters that can restore health. Otherwise the healer will only be treating the symptoms. Such drugs actually take away the person's inner ability to recognise what is right or wrong with their mental state. The drugs that are administered for such patients are successful at numbing their feelings by blocking their

48 The logical aspect is unable to asses and use higher mind principles. The vibrations of the three higher senses have not been established in their logical perceptions.

neural receptors, which simply treats the symptoms. I have seen many mentally ill people walking around in a zombie-like state, not knowing what time of day it was. This is commonly found in mental institutions. Very little is cured, or transformed in such institutionalised state-run hospitals.

The only way to treat the possessed patient in a way that can render permanent cure is for the healer to face the dark force i.e. communicate with it through their higher senses. Then the poltergeist has no place to hide or run because the healer will follow until it is transformed.

Exorcism - dispossessing a house or person

Energy is everywhere, but in various forms. We can listen to the radio because the physical mind has developed a method of decoding the various light wavelengths that produce the sounds that one hears, short and long waves being but two forms of light. Humanity also has a variety of energy frequencies that resonate on various levels of light frequencies (these I term lower), which resonate from the left and higher on the right hemisphere of the brain. These are the logical and intuitive forces of consciousness. The logical aspect is representative of earth energy (time, distance and matter), whereas higher consciousness, which holds the intuitive side, is strongly connected to the universal flow and the laws therein, which are governed by esoterically-based science.

The logical and intuitive forces are but two levels of consciousness that affect everyone's lives in every moment and no one escapes these energies. If you are unaware of the presence of another form of energy, such as a spirit form, you may not hear or even see it. But when you become aware of a presence on a psychic level, such as hearing a sound or even seeing an object move unaided, then it becomes another matter. The healer who has the gifts of inner vision (clairvoyance) and hearing (clairaudience) is able to connect with all forms of energies and the forces that they hold and use. This is because the vibration of the healer will have been finely tuned over many lifetimes, and each lifetime is training where initiations between higher and lower senses occur in order to establish a natural flow between all energy forms and forces therein. Everything you are experiencing now is a preparation for the next lifetime (which is true for all beings).

The healer who works with exorcism is indeed an advanced soul. Not all healers are suited to work with exorcism; there is a specific vibration that is required. For those whose pathway of service is to liberate all souls regardless of which level they resonate on, their gift of exorcism is present and will be used. There is no escaping the preordained path of an exorcist, this recognised quite soon in their life, normally from seven years upwards. There are various forms of exorcism that suit certain forms of energy, and to the experienced healer it is like having a key to open that door. The all-seeing healer has an oversight into all forms of energy. Thought-forms, ghosts, ghouls and poltergeists all have their own particular levels of consciousness - which the exorcist is able to recognise and they then can liberate those trapped by their own energies. For example in certain parts of the tropics the witch doctor can take away dark forces such as curses or implanted demons. In these cultures, the holy person is revered for their magical powers. In the Western parts of the world shaman or priests of earlier civilisations and cultures were relied upon for this type of healing. After the crucifixion of the Master Jesus, the various forms of religious orders took over the shamanic role, and to a great degree utilised their powers to control the sacred acts of exorcism. The various religious orders throughout the Western hemisphere adopted a variety of methods to control the so-called evil of their day. However, many true, gifted healers and visionaries were persecuted, tortured and murdered by sects or larger dominions of religious authorities, all of which has been well documented throughout history. Those gifted healers of earlier times were either deemed to be possessed, or witches, or both by the various religious authorities. Purely because they were able to see and make contact with spirit-beings they were viewed as a threat to authority. History clearly depicts how Christianity used its powers of fear to control the masses from accepting those gifted healers. And if I may add from personal experience, this old consciousness can be found amongst the cultures of today's religious groups - the witch hunt is by no means over.

The religious traditions of prayer and the use of symbolism such as the cross and holy water are common tools used for exorcism by the priest. This method has been handed down through the centuries. Today, it is often the religious priest who is called upon to exhume dark spirits from within houses and sometimes people. This is often quite effective for the lower forms of energy (the less powerful or least intelligent forms of darkness and evil) where the use of religious symbolism and its words often holds enough power to discharge these lower negative forces. On this level I believe that little is seen (clairvoyantly) or heard (clairaudiently) by the priest, but they may intuitively feel a presence. But overall, I believe that most priests are working blindly through their faith with the tools they have. This is not a fault or criticism; it is simply the way that I have experienced it to be.

However, when anyone enters the realms of a stronger darker force such as **the poltergeist,** which carries a higher level of consciousness, it then becomes another matter. The poltergeist is totally aware of how to use their negative forces and powers, and as such is able to bypass all religious symbolism and words is used by the priest in an attempt to excommunicate the dark force. The religious powers have little or no effect upon a superior darker force, because the dark force is able to override them, and as such the negative form of the spirit remains in control. The powers of the priest are then deemed worthless, and the haunting will continue, no matter how much the (logical) willpower of the priest tries to change or challenge those conditions; the effects are the same and the stronger force remains.

Only spirit can move spirit. If the priest is unable to connect clairvoyantly and telepathically with such a negative spirit then there is little chance of a true healing or exorcism taking place. With such dark forces as poltergeists, great awareness and sensitivity are required by the exorcist. The dark powers are cunning and will use every trick to try and undermine the light powers of the healer. When the healer makes contact with the dark force through their higher senses, the healer is able to transform those dark energies in whatever way needed for its total transformation back into the light.

The key for exorcism is that the healer must make contact with the dark force - i.e. the dark force has to be seen by the healer for the right path to be taken and for the cleansing or exorcism to be effective, otherwise the individual is working blindly, and the dark force is able to see and use this for its own gain.

The dark force also communicates with the healer's energies and is therefore also able to read their thoughts, this is known as telepathy. Right from the very beginning of the healing, or even before it commences (as one may plan an exorcism for the next day), there is a battle that rages between the dark and light forces. The dark force knows that the healer is calling and as such can often increase their presence or (as I have experienced) try to block the healer's arrival, possibly by attempting to send the healer in another direction by physically making them go the wrong way. It is right and wise to know that the light will clear the dark if the intentions of the healer are pure at source, where there is no fear. The love vibration will be present and strong and there will be light.

The above is an explanation of the multi-dimensional world that humanity as a whole lives in. In essence everyone is holding the forces of God's creation, the soul and spirit in the crystallised form of the dense physical body, which I refer to as "the human temple". The human form is unique on this level throughout the universe, which is partly why so much emphasis is given to preserving its resonance. But one must never lose sight of the fact that it is the soul that determines when you are to leave this plane of consciousness and also when you are to return as a reincarnated being, i.e. back into the school of life on Mother Earth, one more time. Everything else that has been created around us is given in order to help us grow through the experiences we have attracted. Spiritual values help to guide your lower mind towards higher consciousness development. This is your soul's calling to love and have compassion for all things. The darker forces mentioned throughout this books are misguided, lost and corrupted forms of consciousness that are often unwilling to recognise their own negative aspects. The ego is one of the strongest and most dominating forces at present, fear being the other. But let us not forget that the winds of opportunity are forever blowing; we need only set our sails to be guided through the storms that come.

Other beings and aliens

On this subject, I can only speak in terms relative to my own experience and even then, in a limited manner. This is an area in which little true knowledge exists, but much speculative theory is given. If you believe (rather than deny) that there are other beings in the universe, and that they are superior to man on many levels, then you allow yourself into their field of consciousness. I have had personal experiences with a number of alien beings (as they are loosely termed). The term "alien" is not a true reflection because many beings are supporting global consciousness in an effort to purify the dark ones. Some of the dark aliens that I have been in contact with have been life threatening, whilst others have been gentle, considerate and caring. I will endeavour to explain a couple of such experiences in an effort to ease your minds and alleviate any fears you may have regarding aliens.

The greys: these are beings of the fallen race that once held true vibration of the human being, that of love, peace and joy. As their name suggests their colour (body) is that of *grey tone.* They were a part of the original root race of humanity which inhabited the earth millions of years ago, and as such were a part of the *original evil* that was created due to the development of their ego. The ego is fast approaching its last effort to take control over the universal affairs in relation to the consciousness of earth beings - humans. Greys are discarnate beings that seek ways of entering or possessing a normal human being. They have outlived, and broken their karmic bond with the earth and as such cannot (are not permitted to) incarnate or return through the normal channels. They no longer retain heart feelings, and therefore do not have the distinct quality to love and have compassion for others.

They were banished along with their master by the seven masters of light. Over many thousands of years their influence and powers of possession have continued to decline due to the love vibration of the earth becoming stronger. I would venture to say that there are at present very few (a maximum of three hundred) that are now presently seeking entrance to the earth plane.

Their usual method of possessing a human being is to enter the bedroom at night when an individual is asleep. They seek to enter through the feet, the furthest point from the crown centre. Those who have experienced this may have at first felt some pressure being applied to their feet, which is followed by a clear feeling of a cold energy that passes up along both legs to the knees. This can continue for some time (a number of nights that may be prolonged over a number of months, or even years) in order to break down any resistance that is present from the soul.

Greys always seek full possession and nothing less will do. This is their last desperate attempt to re-establish their race on earth. However, the seven masters are aware of their presence and are overseeing what humanity at large is now doing in order to eradicate them forever. I have personally dealt with two individuals who were in the process of being possessed by greys. In both cases I was able to eradicate them after much soul searching and inner work to find a pathway for the healing to be successful. I have also met an individual who was fully possessed but was clearly aware of another consciousness being present within. At the time of our meeting, the individual was not stressed or worried about the situation, but was in fact quite accepting of it. Maybe it was that person's way of dealing with it, but the individual certainly knew what was happening within.

Beings from other dimensions: there are beings from other dimensions, and by "other dimensions" I mean that they are from another star system and universe. Some are "the good guys" whilst a few are not here to help humanity. There are some destructive alien beings that are more likely to destroy humanity and the environment. I have been in contact with both forms of aliens in a variety of ways. My understanding that comes from these experiences is that there is a galactic war taking place that is based on a very high level of consciousness, which is far too big for the average person – logical thinker – to grasp. Let me explain further:

The good ones: The good aliens have been seeking to raise the consciousness of all human beings for many millennia. Their guidance comes in many forms, such as crop circles which are relevant to what is taking place on earth at present. This group of beings are indeed helping to protect the earth from any negative alien influences. According to my experience, their technology is extremely advanced. Their method of communicating with us is telepathic, and their vision of the world is indeed holistic and balanced. They are caring, loving beings who do not resemble our form; they are much smaller with longer arms and legs. They have little facial structure and their skin is a pastel green. There are areas (landing zones) on this world where these beings land in their craft to make physical contact with certain human beings. This occurs to help establish and possibly confirm that they are real living beings who are compassionate about the continuation of humanity's development towards raising their consciousness. They clearly understand that the human form, in its entirety, is a unique living organism of pure consciousness. It is a consciousness that has an integral role in the continuing development of universal consciousness.

The bad ones: the energy output of the bad aliens is most definitely different from that of the good aliens that I have come across. In my experience, they do not hold a presence of stillness or calmness; I can hear and feel them coming. When I have been in the presence of their energy I have wanted to move as far away as possible, but of course it is never quite like that. If anyone finds that it is their path to work with transforming such forces, they have to be fully present, and without fear of any kind.

I have experienced that many such aliens create portholes as entrance points from one dimension to another. These are simply ways of getting in and out of the earth's energy field. Such portals are invisible to the physical eye and are at times not visible to the clairvoyant eye. There is a technique (the third eye) that can pick up their vibration in order to fully detect their presence. The universal force that protects the earth is like a firewall that protects your computer from invading cookies, spam or viruses. To a very great degree it is effective. Sometimes a rogue alien can get in, but is soon detected (by masters and master healers alike) and transformed.

All negative alien beings are here to use and abuse in order to try and control and even take life. Sometimes, certain types of aliens do not respond to the normal practice of removal by exorcism. However there are other means, but I cannot share such insight with you. I respect the laws that I have been shown and given by higher masters in relation to this subject and must remain silent.

However if this is your chosen pathway, you will be given adequate tools for the work at hand. You will be protected and guided, as I have been, which is also true regarding the earth-bound exorcism. Whenever this work is given to you, you will be able to meet it fully in order to transform whatever vibration may come into your path. Always remember that the pathway is there and ready for those whose form of service follows this line of work. The experiences and discoveries that will come with this level of serving will astound and uplift the soul, time and time again.

Chapter 11

Methods of Protection from Dark Forces

Anything negative I refer to as a dark force. This is because whenever you respond to an experience in a negative manner it can develop and grow into something very destructive. For example, violence is commonly portrayed on the TV, which I feel has a negative influence upon the values of life. This can erode and distort your values of life - which could happen subconsciously - to the degree where the meaning of life is negated.

The mystique that the dark side emanates is often attractive for those who are curious and adventurous. Many get lured into practicing black magic because of the pleasingly instant results that often accompany it. But be aware, this is an illusion that is created by the dark side in order to entice you into its threshold. This is extremely difficult to step out of or to transform once the dark side has a hold on the psyche. My advice is to trust your heart feeling - if something does not feel right, simply walk away from it and do not be tempted. Look beyond it for greater clarity and truth.

What is exorcism?

There is much fear around this word, due to certain factors such as movies which tend to portray the negative side of exorcism as a form of true power, when in fact it is not. The art of exorcism is a true power because it transforms the negative to give new life and meaning to what is being transformed. I call it an art because it is an ability that few have. The exorcist seeks to transform all evil forms, it is their life calling. It is not something that anyone can learn to do from a book; it is an individual soul calling (one is born to be an exorcist) that has a depth that reaches far beyond logical reasoning and fear. The soul and human being that works with exorcism is an advanced soul who carries no fear in any part of their psyche. They are true *spiritual warriors* who are able to transform any negative force, regardless of its powers. It is also true to say that the exorcist or healer who undertakes such work carries no darkness within themselves, the vibration is simply not there. If any form of darkness was present within such a healer it would not be possible for him/her to serve the light by transforming dark forces. All healers who work in this field carry a deep sense of love and light within their whole being and are doing the work of the creator.

There are a number of positive ways of blocking and stopping dark negative forces from affecting your energy fields. I will highlight these in accordance with the specific energy that seeks to cast a shadow over your soul. But firstly I would like to make it clear that your positive thinking, truth and light force are all important keys to prevent any shadow from falling upon you. With this insight, let us move forward.

Responsibility: whatever you experience in life you have attracted to yourself on some level. If you recognise and accept this truth, then you will become more present in any given situation. An important aspect to understand here is that not every negative force (for example, an angry person that comes to you) is seeking to destroy, control or influence you in a negative manner. The energy - anger - may actually be seeking a path into the light, and you (for whatever reason) may be the person who is holding that inner awareness to take it into the light. Your light may be of the right frequency for the angers to be transformed. This will demonstrate itself by the manner in which you react to the anger. If, for example, you do not react in a negative manner but accept the anger and ask yourself *Why am I experiencing this now?* Then you may have a different experience that will give an opportunity to transform the anger. In other words you attract the experience to help take you further into the light of truth and love.

The most important aspect of protectionism and the transformation of any dark forces is to hold no fear. Otherwise the protection and transformational properties of your light force towards the darkness will have an element of doubt, which is a weakness. There can be no such weakness when dealing with negative forces. You must be truly present in your light in order to hold its force, if not you are in danger of becoming lost due to some fear entering your consciousness. Yes, the key is the universal light that is the core energy of your seed of life, your soul.

Judgement of another: this I feel is the most common form of energy that darkness uses to separate individuals and groups. Have you ever felt a strong negative force of someone's dislike of you in your workplace, amongst your family or in society? The answer is most likely a resounding yes! Why is judgement such a negative force? The answer is simple; judgement is purely ego-based. The ego creates separation for its own identity; therefore it is not of the light. Judgement is not a universal law. There is no justification for judgement because the whole picture of any event or happening is never completely understood. For example, our preferences create separation; whenever you say to yourself "I like this, not that," or "I don't like you because of the clothes you wear," or "it is your fault, look at what you have done," this is separation through judgemental attitudes, because you cannot love when you judge another.

I remember on one occasion, many years ago, I was standing on a street in my home town with a friend, watching the world go by. My friend suddenly said, "Hey Ralph, look over there," as he pointed across the street to the other side of the road.

"Look at her hair, what a mess." My sight became focused on other people walking along the other side of the road. I tried to figure out who he was referring to. I sensed his dislike and felt his anger at what he was pointing at. As I fixed my sight to where he was pointing, I noticed a young woman walking along the street whose hair was bright green in colour.

My friend continued to complain and said, "Who does she think she is?"

My reply to him was "You cannot judge her by the colour of her hair."

My friend uttered a few more words of disapproval as he felt that I had disagreed with his point of view, we then parted company. Some thirty minutes later I was walking along the same street when the woman with the green hair was walking towards me. I thought to myself *I must stop and ask her*. I ventured towards her and stopped her in a kind manner and asked why her hair was such a colour. She looked at me for a moment as her face opened with a smile (as if she had been asked this question a thousand time before) and replied. "Oh,

I am an actress in the theatre, and at present I am acting in a child's pantomime which requires my hair to be this colour."

At that moment I had a big sense of acknowledgment within myself as I thanked her for sharing this. I later told my friend what I had discovered about the green hair mystery. His response was initially one of denial by saying, "It was a mess anyway," but deep down I knew he had grown a little through his misguided judgement.

People often have a good heart but still judge because they believe they are right, it is a way of justification that serves no one, except the ego. Judgement is old consciousness (3D) at work which no longer serves the human race, just as choice does not. Choice and judgement are like brother and sister; they are of the same essence. Nothing is ever black or white, just as there is no right or wrong; there is the experience. Any experience can only be fully realised when you are fully present. And when you are fully present, past experiences cannot interfere because of your acceptance of the moment, and when you accept judgement cannot be present.

Whenever you project your thoughts as forms of judgement upon another human being they feel it through their psychic abilities. Words do not have to be spoken because the consciousness has actively reached that person, the one you are mentally focused on. If you feel that someone is or has judged you (for whatever reason) there are positive steps that can be taken to transform your own feelings about it, and not the other way around. The first thing to realise is that change can only come from within you. It is seldom possible to change another person's direction. One positive step that will take you out of the ego's trap is to learn not to take any judgement of you personally. When you do this, you automatically stop feeding the negative energy. This is because ego-based judgement requires energy through the feedback it gets. This only occurs if you take the judgement personally; it will feel your response just as surely as you will have felt its projection towards you. By not taking the judgement personally, you are effectively stepping out of the box (logic and emotion) and into the circle of life, your higher consciousness. From within the circle you can ask the question of why you are being judged. In that moment you are taking your own responsibility towards the judgement which will help you understand yourself better through your own intentions as well as the one judging you. For example, the one who is judging you may be repeating a similar pattern with others. This could be for many reasons, one being self-justification or playing the power game.

If you take any form of judgement personally you will become lost in the drama or in victimhood, which only serves to feed the negative source. On the other hand, by not taking it personally you will come back to your natural flow of self-trust by remaining in your power, your light and truth. The person who is judging you will feel your positive response and may not bother you again because they feel that they cannot influence you in any way. Then the one who judges will have to look at why they judge. Another way to deal with judgement is to challenge it directly through thoughts and actions. When people are confronted (the mirror effect) by you asking, "What's the problem?" they will do one of two things; they will either stay in denial or attack. Both are not of the truth. Denial is used as a tool to run away from responsibility, whereas attack is anger-based and is trying to defend the ego's investment in its identity. When you are being judged, you will intuitively know which course of action is necessary - listen to it. In this manner you will be seeking the truth because no one person has the right to judge another!

Two forms of thought projection (towards you) that you may face could be hate or jealousy. Both are strong, negative dark forces that arise from the caldron of the emotions. However there are two effective methods to block their projection, one being the mirror effect and the other the wall.

The mirror effect: if you believe that someone is trying to influence you with negative thoughts you can imagine that you are standing in a circle of mirrors. The mirrors are effective in reflecting those thought forms back to the one who sends them whilst at the same time you are fully present to receive all positive thoughts. This is a non-invasive method of protection.

The wall effect: another form of protection which I have found to be successful is the *wall method.* Let's say, for example, that there is someone in your office who keeps stepping into your space by trying to influence you psychically. When this happens to you next time get yourself to focus for a moment on the individual concerned. Then build an imaginary wall between you both. Try to imagine this with your inner eye or through the third eye. This wall will stop the negative projection whilst at the same time you will be able to see and converse with that person as freely as they are with you. That person may feel that something has changed, but can be unsure of what has changed or how. That person may then stop their game playing with you and move on.

To go a bit deeper, other negative thought projections are often used and practiced in many regions of the world, curses being one. In the West, black witches use their powers by placing a curse on someone they may dislike or see as a threat to their power. Intention is everything in life. Light beings and healers are often sought after (by those affected by dark forces) to transform any negative forces that may be affecting an individual or a group of people in their home or life.

I was once asked to go to a house where strange happenings took place overnight, such as sounds and movements being heard where there was no one present. I went along as soon as I could. On arrival I entered the house to be confronted by a heavy depressing energy. The owner of the house said that the disturbances were occurring upstairs in a particular bedroom. I immediately began to check each bedroom out, starting with where the owner had heard the most disturbances. It was true, there was a dark energy in that particular room, but I did not find its connection to the source. I then moved my scanning (mental telepathy) to the ground floor and I physically entered the large living room. I immediately picked up on an object that stood next to the TV. The outer appearance of the object (a wax cathedral) looked very beautiful, but I could see and feel its evil. I asked the owner, "Where did you get that from?"

"Strange you should ask, I was in town two days ago and this woman, a stranger to me, offered it for free. She seemed so kind and had a nice face so I accepted it and brought it home."

I informed her that the object was cursed by the woman whom I believed to be a black witch. I then stated, "She gave you this ornament for one reason only, and that was to give her access into your home on a psychic level, this is how they work."

It is often a very effective way for dark forces to gain entrance into a dwelling. I immediately took the object out of the house and transformed it back to the light and the curse was lifted. The owner was shocked by my explanation, but she then realised that she had suspected in the first moment of meeting this stranger - that there was something strange about the woman - but she had not listened to her intuition. This was a lesson well learned.

On the African continent, I understand (through patient experience) that placing a curse on someone is commonly practiced. Witch doctors have a strong influence in this area, and are even paid to lay a curse just as they are paid to remove curses laid upon individuals. There is much fear around such curses, which I feel is due to the strong active belief system that has been built around them for generations.

I have experienced on countless occasions the transformation of both incarnate and discarnate dark beings. Some have been black witches who have sought my help to transform them from being on the path of darkness onto the path of light service to others. If you happen to have crossed the path of a black witch in a negative manner, for whatever reason, they will seek to repay you tenfold with their evil ways. On one occasion I was working to transform - cleanse - a sacred place from being used by a coven of witches, which was an assembly of thirteen incarnate black witches. I was deep into the work when a thirteenth century discarnate black witch appeared to try to stop my light work. She was a powerful spirit who had been summoned by the coven to do some of their evil work. She tried to influence me with her black magic and sorcery, which had no effect on my being. I then duly removed her by sending her to the light for transformation.

On another occasion, a dark war lord sought my help to be transformed from his ways of destruction. He was not feeling well within himself and had realised that he wanted to change his ways after so many lifetimes of serving the dark side. He wanted to become a light worker. At our very first meeting he asked me, "Do you really want to help me?"

I said, "Of course. Why not? This is my pathway in life."

He then informed me that the three previous healers who had tried to help him had died. I informed him that I held no fear in my body and that I would indeed help him. He seemed pleased at my resolve. On gaining access into his past lives I understood the depth of his darkness and why he had become tired of destroying rather than creating. I worked with this strong soul for a number of months, and that led to a peaceful ending. I believe that peace of mind and heart was what he was seeking, as well being able to step back into the ray of light to be with his true soul being.

Spirit beings are all around us; some are here to visit and some are here to serve. They cannot be directly seen by physical sight because their body vibration is higher than that of the vibration of physical light. At times their presence can be sensed in the form of feeling the room temperature suddenly drop and become colder. It is quite common to feel the presence of a spirit as a gentle breeze passing by. Another way that a spirit being will disclose its presence is by producing the scent of a flowery perfume when there are no flowers present in the room. This is a calling card of spirit.

For a spirit to be present in a room or a séance meeting, it must be connected to the soul because the spirit is the server of the soul. This is apparent whenever I have given mediumistic messages in séances. The soul manifests the spiritual light to form the appearance of a metaphysical body of energy. This is purely so that the person - spirit form - will be recognised by the one who it has come to connect with. The connection may be to a relative, which is a common happening in such gatherings. The medium can give a clear description of the spirit present, which often includes a name, the type of clothes worn or even how they died. The soul can even manifest pain in the medium's body to indicate how it died, such as with a strong heart pain. There is always a celebration on the spiritual realm when true communication takes place between the realms. I have experienced the spiritual world to be similar in many respects to earth. On earth, humans have characteristics that help define their character. Some people are serious whilst others are not, some may be mischievous and others more dry. These characteristics are not lost when the soul and spirit leave the body during the physical transformation of what we call death. When I channel to give a messages from a loved one the other side, I often describe their physical appearance and an aspect of their character. At times I feel and act or behave as they may have; this is simply a means of greater proof of who is making contact. This is all true and well when the séance is held by an experienced medium. But even here I have experienced mischievous spirits who have come to play games to disrupt the séance. This is normally quickly recognised and dealt with by the medium. Usually the communication to a spirit being will appear in a body form and clothes that will be recognised by the receiver of the message. This is in order that a deeper connection between them will be established. Then the vibration between the three, that of the spirit, the medium (mediator) and the third party (the relative or friend of the spirit) will be established. It is a beautiful and natural means of joining the realms. The initiate who is developing their three higher senses through such means as creative visualisation meditation, will actually experience a degree of the paranormal and metaphysical realities that cannot be explained logically. These are the mediumistic skills I refer to here.

As I mentioned earlier, there are spirit helpers and guides in both realms (heaven and earth). So let us take a look at both:

Spirit helper: these come to develop their gifts connected to a previous life on earth. The spirit may have been a doctor or a surgeon and may appear during a healing session to offer their service by, for example, helping to transform the etheric energy that is connected to an injury or an organ. They may even appear in your life to help support you through a crisis of some kind.

Spiritual helpers are not directly fixed to any individual; they may come and go at will. I have known of some to be working with a number of spiritual helpers at the same time. This is why I refer to them (with due respect) as "floating helpers" because they are not bound to any particular person, they seek to serve wherever needed.

Main guides: each individual has a main guide that has travelled to earth with them. The guide is specifically for you and if, for example, you have not yet connected to your main guide, the guide is waiting for you to open the door to your spiritual realms. As your higher faculties (senses) develop it is possible and natural for you to seek your soul connection to your main guide. This is normally achieved through meditation practice by asking for your connection or channel to be opened to your main guide. This is why it is important to understand

and use the *law of demand* in order to access answers from spirit, otherwise the universe cannot respond without your consent to access greater wisdom. Your main guide is present and waiting for your spiritual development to reach a vibration that will open the door, this is its soul task. When such an opening begins to vibrate, you may at first only see an outline of a being, but by gradually increasing your body-soul vibration you will raise your energies into higher consciousness, from where greater clarity and connection will be achieved. From this platform the main guide may guide you to different realms in order to experience teachings from higher beings and possibly from other worlds and dimensions. This has been chiefly my experience throughout my spiritual development. I have never had an earth master or guru. My guidance has always been from higher spiritual sources. This is my truth, it may not be yours. It is important that you follow your own truth and intuition without fear.

Your main guide will be with you for as long as your teaching remains at a certain level - that level being the establishment of your 4D consciousness. It is wise to remember that your chakra work and their vibrations are critical in aiding your transformational inner work. Each vibration has to be mastered to form a unified collective vibration in order that the whole self, physical, spirit and soul are in harmony with each other. It may take a whole lifetime (or longer) to reach that pinnacle with your main guide. However when you have reached that higher point of establishing the consciousness of 4D, the main guide will no longer have the purpose of serving you and will depart. The departure of your main guide may be a strong experience for you (as it was for me) because you will have created a strong bond. Such a bond would have included, in part, you seeing the world through the main guide's eyes. But it is wise to remember that dependency is not a criterion that any true spiritual being aspires to. A part of everyone's transformation from the 3D into the 4D is learning to stand in their own power of light, but in a collective manner.

From my personal experience, making contact with your main guide is an important step towards receiving your master guidance!

The dark side: the vast majority of beings present in any given location are of the light. However, it must be said that on the journey of seeking your spirit helper, guides and masters, clarity of thought and feelings are of key importance whilst you are looking to establish a connection to either of the levels mentioned. For me, clarity is about how balanced the lower nature is and how developed the higher senses are. By freeing yourself of fear and emotional disturbances, your vibration will rise to aid your communication with spirit and higher beings on a telepathic clairvoyant level. Spirit is already there because they resonate on the higher dimensions. They know what you are feeling and thinking. It is up to the initiate to raise their vibration in order to gain access into the higher vibration of light. The inner work of transforming fears and emotions are of great importance for your spiritual development.

There are also false helpers, guides and masters in this realm just as there are on the physical level. You may ask how it is possible if they are of spirit. But you may also ask the same question about earth beings because they are also of spirit and have a soul too. Basically, the energy is the same for humans as it is for spirit; it is a force that carries consciousness because we are ultimately conscious beings regardless of the dimension on which we resonate.

The key word here is *intent.* What are the intentions behind any thought you may have? Your intentions coincide with any control issues you may have, just as they do with the liberating qualities. So who controls what and how? A false spirit (not true to the light) can pretend to be of the light in order to gain access into the initiate's psyche. I have known guides to appear in a blaze of light, only to find that they were not of the light. I have known guides to come to initiates and promise them rewards, only to find that they had been fooled in the belief that all spirit energies were meant to be true and of the light. At present there seems to be an increase in consciousness rising, meaning that there are more who are seeking to be true and are in search of guidance and wisdom of spiritual affairs.

The greater the light, the harder the dark forces will try to interfere with its vibration. This is a natural phenomenon. Which is true (to an extent) of the initiate who is seeking deeper spiritual development. However I must say do not let this alarm you, because the greater majority of those who are in transition are not affected by the dark phenomenon that I speak of here. Each and every one is being protected by their light; I am merely trying to demonstrate to you possibilities not probabilities. In this manner you will at least be aware and prepared on a certain level to deal with a negative experience that may come to you regarding this matter. As an example I will say that if you have a spiritual ego then you are more likely to be corrupted, or certainly influenced, by dark forces. As an example your guide may come to you and show itself to be a certain master or angel. You may be so overwhelmed by its presence that your ego will override your ability (feelings and intuition) to detect anything that may be abnormal. One of the true tests of detecting if a spirit is true to the light is if the spirit begins to demand anything of you, such as telling you to "Go and tell this person what I say to do." Or they may tell you to phone a friend to warn them of something. The dark force cannot help itself from not trying to control you, your life and your psyche. As with all dark forces that manipulate others there is always a payback time! A true light being or spirit will never demand anything of you; it will not interfere with your choices, unless asked to. Any light worker is there to help guide you through the labyrinth of life towards developing an inner faith in yourself and the universe. It is not in any true guide's consciousness to control you. They leave you to make your own choices and decisions, as well as mistakes. They will not interfere with your inner process unless asked to by you; otherwise they may be preventing necessary experiences. And even then there are times when a guide will refuse to help, because they may see what you cannot, and use their wisdom accordingly.

The method of protecting yourself from all false spirit beings is to enact the *sacred law of protection.* This law must be used whilst initiating, that is until you trust the guidance you are receiving on this level, or until you have reached a level of consciousness whereby no dark force can enter your space under disguise. Most false spirits are harmless and seek to play rather than create negative energies, but it must also be said that some do create negativity! As an example, I would like to share what my own initiation was like when I was guided to give the sacred law of protection by a master.

The example: whilst I was teaching and guiding a group of mediators, one person got in touch with a guide. This person (let's call him John) was unable to describe the guide clearly, but he felt safe that the guide was in his presence. John felt sure that it was a good spirit and was told by the spirit guide that he had come to help him on his spiritual path. All seemed to go well for a number of weeks during his meditations, but then John intuitively felt that something was wrong although he could not put his finger on what was bothering him. His vision of the guide was not clear due to an imbalance in the emotional and third-eye chakras, which created fear about his own abilities to see and be guided. John told me that the guide had begun to ask him to do certain things, which seemed to go against spirituality, like separating himself from the meditative group. He was becoming insecure about his guide and asked me to check him out during the next meditation, which I did on a one to one basis.

During this meditation I observed the guide standing next to John, but a little to the back on his left side. It was a Native American Indian, of the Sioux tribe. I detected a shadow to one side of the guide's energy field and my suspicions arose. After the meditation had finished I asked John to come back the next day for a private sitting to sort the guide issue out. He agreed and he duly arrived the next day at noon. We entered the meditation room and we began to enter the meditative state, a deeper state of consciousness in order to seek spiritual guidance. I once again saw the guide appear behind John. I was now seeking guidance on how to challenge the spirit being that was with John. I had informed John to simply focus on the light as he had asked for the guide to appear. In those moments the words *If you are who you say you are, show yourself in the true light* came to me and I was told by my own guide to repeat this three times to the spirit that was with John. On my third round of repeating these sacred words at the end of *Show yourself in the true light,* the spirit changed form and became another Native American, but it was a dark force. I then challenged it and asked it why it had come to fool

John. The false guide told me that it wanted to control John; it was a power game because he wanted to be a chief. At that moment a true light worker came to take the false guide away. From what I was told by my own guide, the false guide would have much work to do to transform the negative to be a light worker.

I explained to John what had happened. He stepped back within himself and looked frightened at the realisation that he had been fooled by a spirit being. I tried to reassure him that this was not a common happening and that he should continue with his meditation practice with the knowledge that he now had a tool of protection that he could use at any given moment. Now I have shared this method of protection - *If you are who you say you are, show yourself in the true light* which must be repeated three times for it to be activated - you have a universal law of protection against false spirits.

Your Master: your true master is one of seven masters of creation. Each soul on earth has a specific soul connection to one of the seven masters. Their vibration is carried and held by you and your directive to serve others through your gifts - this why you are here on earth. Each soul is a seed of light, a being of expansive consciousness, that of love, light peace and joy. All human beings are helped and guided by spirit helpers, guides and masters regardless of whether they are conscious of it or not. Ultimately this is everyone's pathway in life, to serve for the greater good.

However I have also known that some have been tricked or fooled into believing that they have made contact with their master, when in fact it was a negative force pretending to be a master. With false guides and masters, one of the main difficulties for the initiate is to see sprit forms clearly, which requires the development of the higher senses. If, for example, the third eye is underdeveloped, then clarity or clear vision of the guide or master will be limited, which can lead to errors being made. In such a case as in many other situations it is important to listen to your intuition and trust it! Even if your insight is not so clear, it is important to challenge a spirit that you feel is false, with the words of protection and send it back into the light. All spirit forms recognise our fears and imperfections, but with the right intent the law of protection is true. In fact, I have known negative spirits that have come to me because they are seeking release from the dark side. In this respect not all negative, dark or evil forces appear to harm, they may simply be seeking a way through their own darkness to transform it and to stand in the light.

Negative spirits in a house or dwelling: a negative spirit is often felt as anything that disturbs the peace and tranquillity of a house or dwelling. Such disturbances could be explained as hearing sounds or noises in a certain area of a house where no one is present. This is commonly experienced as footsteps or a door opening and closing. One may hear music being played or a bad smell may appear for no apparent reason. Quite suddenly you may feel a certain chill in the room or the lights may flicker. These are some of the sensations that are felt through the physical senses demonstrating that there is a spiritual presence. There are a number of reasons why a negative spirit may appear. For example, the energy may be attached to the building because it lived there whilst alive on earth and was unable to let go of it when physical death came due to its attachment to the building. Some dark forces choose a house to try and control the occupants, usually through fear. There are stronger spirit forces such as the poltergeist for example. The poltergeist has the knowledge to move items or write on mirrors, all of which I have personally seen and worked with to transform. I have also come to understand that negative spirits use energy lines (leylines) to travel along. If your house is located along such a line then I recommend that you seek expert help to establish if that energy line is clean and clear and holds positive energy.

It must also be said that there are times when a negative spirit may actually seek the light in order to be transformed. This must be kept in mind because not every negative force seeks to destroy or create mischief whenever it may appear to you. When the three higher senses are active and clear, the healer is able to communicate with that energy in order to get a deeper understanding of why it has appeared. Depending on what the energy is, the experienced exorcist will remove the negative force and transform the space it has occupied to create a light space.

Summary

Every being on earth is here to raise their consciousness, which will create greater harmony and wellbeing. Harmony creates peace within you. By having a balanced chakra system, where all chakras are resonating on a similar vibration, peace and harmony can be established. When this is achieved, an opening and development of the three higher senses will occur naturally. Clairvoyance (the third eye), clairaudience (the throat) and clairsentience (the crown chakra) will become more active. The correct development of the three higher senses gives greater access and understanding to the universal forces, laws and rules that collectively demonstrate life on all dimensions to the initiate. Through the development and use of the higher senses you will begin to understand and experience the insights that the fourth and fifth dimensions provide.

The paranormal and metaphysical properties of the universal life force flow through all human beings. For example, the appearance of a spirit form in a room is a paranormal happening which can be witnessed by the initiate through the third eye. It is the same vibration that opens the door to visualise the aura and chakras, which are metaphysical in nature. In other words, through raising the vibration from 3D to 4D, the initiate is able to go beyond the limitations of the five physical senses. This is a natural transition for all human beings to seek and follow. When these forms of insight are established within, no negative, dark or evil force can dominate or influence your being.

Conclusion

With the explanations of the dark forces within this book it would be wise to remember that your inner light, the very nature of your whole being, that seed, is the ultimate repellent of any dark force. Fear is the enemy of the soul because it is of the dark side and cannot coexist within anyone without it being the dominant aspect. It is here that we find many troubled souls seeking release from negative forces such as fear. But I repeat that the responsibility is to be pure in mind, heart and body. It is ultimately up to you as an individual to be focused and present on the positive aspect of your life, because each and every one of us is a collective force of love and light.

The human being has reached a critical point in evolution in which there is great opportunity to transform the ego and the darkness created by it. The universal messages (channelled insight, astrological quarters, Mayan calendar) are repeating the same message - there is no tomorrow, only NOW, act now do not wait. Many are waking to the fact that there is a sacred path that requires no sacrifice of any sort, but simply asks that each and every one of us dedicates their lives towards disciplining mind and emotion through the study and experience of following a sacred spiritual path. In this manner you will discover, or at the very least find the sacred will through which true initiations of light consciousness can take place within you. This is the only reason why you have returned to the earth, reincarnation after reincarnation.

The light consciousness that emanates from the earth penetrates other universes and star systems. We, you and I are part of its expansion as the earth's consciousness continues to develop in a positive manner. Why else do other beings have such an interest in our safety and well-being? Within the seed of human consciousness there is held a key to eternal life that others wish to accomplish and have – it is called **LOVE!**

Have you got the message yet? NO! Why? Because the human race has not (as yet) followed the fundamental law of *love thy neighbour.* Humans have not yet learned to get on with each other, because our so-called differences are getting in the way of our love for each other as brother and sister! NOW IS THE TIME!

This is not an end to this book but rather a beginning of another page and chapter, just as your life is never at an end; it is the beginning of an end. I would recommend that no one should struggle with the thought of death, because it is simply a rebirth into another state of consciousness. This is what the human being is struggling so hard to understand. The spiritual path will never be found by logic alone, because the vibration of loving wisdom is far beyond logic.

All it takes is your permission to make the necessary changes to your life in order to free yourself once and for all from your fears, the ego's control, and the darkness that accompanies it! This is my truth, there is no more or less to it than that, just your permission to say yes to the eternal light within!

Blessings to each and every being,
love and light,
Ralph.

Book recommendation

I recommend the book "Sensitelligent - a guide to Life" to help you transform any negative aspect you may be holding. The book provides valuable insight of the negative and positive aspects of the human nature. It gives practical guidance to understand how fears are created and how to transform them. It also illustrates ways in which your fears may be controlling you, and how to apply the many positive bridging actions given, such as "I trust" in order to transform your fears. The book's depth of truth and clarity complements its simplicity. There is also a reference section in the book that gives deeper knowledge to specific areas of life, such as "Being present" or "Thoughts" which can be applied more deeply to all aspects of life. The book will help guide you to understand how to listen more deeply to your inner-being, how to develop your trust in order to raise your consciousness above fear and control.

You can read more about the Sensitelligent concept on www.sensitelligent.com.

I wish you joy, love and light on your journey.
Ralph K. Jenkins

About the Author

 I am a student of life who continually seeks Universal wisdom. I have the ability to see many forms of energy that go beyond physical boundaries, such as the metaphysical. These gifts enable me to connect and interact with many of the life forces that the physical eye cannot see and logic cannot reason with. I explore through these insights the links between Metaphysics and various sciences, such as Astrophysics, Quantum mechanics, Physiology and Pathology of the body. All of these are, in my opinion, linked to the essence of life.

I am guided to direct the awareness I have been entrusted with to help others, and continually seek opportunities to communicate those spiritual experiences with others through mutual dialogue.

Energy is often talked about but not felt or experienced in concrete ways. In the light of this I have created a variety of lectures, seminars, courses and workshops as a means to create greater understanding of Universal Laws.

You can read more about my work at the following websites:

www.verusanimus.com
www.sensitelligent.com
www.pilipala.se

Lightning Source UK Ltd.
Milton Keynes UK
23 February 2011
168111UK00001B/3/P